Praise for *Sexual Enlightenment*

"Freddy Zental and Elsbeth are two of the most spiritually skillful people at bringing an untainted teaching and practice of the ancient art of Tantra to Western shores, showing us how informed sex supports not only our innate longing for union, but also our overall well-being."
~ Dr. Michael Bernard Beckwith, Author of *Life Visioning*

"Sexual Enlightenment is an essential guidebook, beautifully written and grounded in the human need for attaining the greatest capacity for joy, love and mutual care. Elsbeth and Freddy Zental direct us into the kind of mindset that allows for being at choice in how to use our sexual energy, our greatest life force, to bring forth effective action in attaining true intimacy, not only with ourselves, but in creating our lives and relationships in authentic fulfillment."
~ Jan Smith, Founder and President of Center for Authentic Leadership, Inc. – *Creating and leading fulfilling lives from your unique gifts*

"Freddy and Elsbeth are excellent teachers in the new age of sexual consciousness. Their book will enlighten you to the possibilities of transforming normal sex to a spiritual art form. Through wisdom, woven together with real life stories, you will learn about sexual energy, removing its blocks and discovering its ecstasy."
~ Charles Muir, Director Source School of Tantra & Co-Author of *Tantra: The Art of Conscious Loving*

"In this remarkable book, Elsbeth and Freddy Zental share a profoundly important and liberating insight: that sexual life force energy—the fundamental spark of life itself—can be harnessed to ignite our creativity, open our hearts, light up our lives and illuminate our souls. Based on their groundbreaking work with thousands of individuals and couples over the past decade, they show us, with simple yet powerful practices, how we can consciously direct this primal power to realize the birthright of every human being, a life full of joy, creativity, pleasure and love."
~ Neal Rogin, Author and Filmmaker, *The Awakening Universe*

"I have experienced Elsbeth and Freddy Zental 'up-close and personal' and their healing practice and teachings of TantraNova® are the real deal. *Sexual Enlightenment* provides a significant new approach to creating harmony and balance within us by raising our consciousness and putting it into a daily practice. Blending ancient wisdom with practical holistic intimacy exercises, this book will empower you to experience a deep knowing of compassion . . . a sensitive art and science that is so necessary for the evolution of our consciousness in today's world."

> ~ Dr. Darren R. Weissman, Best Selling Author of *The Power of Infinite Love & Gratitude* and Developer of *The LifeLine Technique*®

"It takes devotion to live a beloved relationship as well as teach the practices of relating and loving through Tantra. Elsbeth and Freddy have stood the test of time. They radiate the gifts of this consciousness for loving. *Sexual Enlightenment* is like reaching for heaven on earth and finding it in the eyes of one another. Praises to these two devoted beings of love."

> ~ Caroline Muir, Author of *Tantra Goddess, A Memoir of Sexual Awakening* & Co-Author of *Tantra: The Art of Conscious Loving*

"Freddy and Elsbeth have dedicated their lives to assisting singles, couples, gay, straight and everyone in between awaken to their inherent sexual power and inner beauty – to return to spiritual wholeness. As regular workshop leaders at Bodhi Spiritual Center I have experienced the depth of their teachings firsthand and therefore find this book most timely and important. Praise for this work and congratulations to you who are reading it - you are blessed."

> ~ Mark Anthony Lord, Author of *Though Shall Not Suffer - Seven Steps to a Life of Joy!* Founder/Spiritual Director of Bodhi Spiritual Center, Chicago

"Creativity, focus, energy, greater health, longevity, passion, presence, strong relationships, pleasure, spiritual awakening, love, and joy emerge from the practices of sexual consciousness. Let's learn them all from these gifted authors."

> ~ Linda Bloom, Co-Author of *101 Things I Wish I Knew When I Got Married: Simple Lessons to Make Love Last* and *Secrets of Great Marriages: Real Truths from Real Couples about Lasting Love*

Sexual Enlightenment

How to Create Lasting Fulfillment in Life, Love, and Intimacy

ELSBETH MEUTH
FREDDY ZENTAL WEAVER

BALBOA
PRESS
A DIVISION OF HAY HOUSE

Balboa Press books may be ordered through booksellers or by contacting:

Balboa Press
A Division of Hay House
1663 Liberty Drive
Bloomington, IN 47403
www.balboapress.com
1 (877) 407-4847

Printed in the United States of America.

ISBN: 978-1-4525-8543-7 (sc)
ISBN: 978-1-4525-8544-4 (e)

Library of Congress Control Number: 2013919076

Balboa Press rev. date: 11/14/2013

Release
the Day
Therapeutic Massage

Rosa Casas,
NCTMB

96 Roosevelt Street
St. Charles IL 60174

630-234-5855

To the conscious evolving of humanity

To Rosa —
keep loving, creating
and enjoying!

Bekka & Todd Bstot

Contents

Acknowledgments

We are deeply grateful for the support and encouragement we received from our extended community in bringing this book to bear.

In particular we wish to thank Freddy Zental's father, Fred Weaver, MD, who not only greatly impacted his son through his work on *Creative Self-Discovery* but has played the role of advisor for us in developing TantraNova.

Not until later in life did Elsbeth recognize the enormous impact her late father made on her by imparting a sense of entrepreneurship and business acumen. She is filled with infinite gratitude for the role model he provided for her.

We are deeply grateful to Charles Muir, who guided us in deepening our tantric learning and prepared us for birthing TantraNova. His contribution to and influence on our work and this book is immeasurable. We are most appreciative of Caroline Muir and her gracious initiation of Elsbeth into the world of the divine feminine.

Deep appreciation goes to Dr. Fernando Flores for his work on *Communication for Action* and ontological design that influenced Elsbeth in a profound way while working with him. This set the foundation for rigor and clarity that she has been applying to her personal life, her teaching, and her leading the TantraNova institute. We thank Jan Smith from the bottom of our hearts for her work on authentic leadership, which has greatly impacted our work at TantraNova.

Many thanks go to Marc Beth for the superb guidance and skillful recording in putting the audio practices together (available online via the Practice Section in Part III of this book); Haans Peterson for catching the spirit of the TantraNova practices through his artwork; and our writer, Elise Vaz, at Arbor Books, who guided us tirelessly in the proposal and manuscript process, called us into chiseling away on our message to come to the essence of what we wanted to share, and helped us convey it with clarity.

We treasure the input, contribution or feedback to our manuscript by friends, family, colleagues, and associates: Jonas Binder, Mildred Davis, Michael Grygleski, Todd Jones, Constantina Karathanasis, Wanda Knight, Christine Krumsee, Danute Kuncas, Jane Lewis, Esther Meuth-Binder, Rossitza Mircheva, Kathleen Peterson, Jeffrey Spahn, Steven Tyler, Dr. Barbara Vertel, Saul Zenkevicius, Lauren Zerbst, and many more who enriched our work with their reflections.

Working with our support team at Balboa Press was a great experience: their steadfastness, handholding, guidance, and encouragement were most welcome. Thanks to all of you and in particular to Adriane Pontecorvo.

Last not least, we thank the participants of our seminars, retreats, and private programs for their openness and the trust they granted us throughout their participation at TantraNova. Each of you has contributed to us so we could become better teachers, more humble human beings, and the catalysts that we are meant to be.

Introduction

It was the summer of 1969. Freddy, an African American in his early teens, was sprawled across the deck of the family houseboat in Sausalito, California, the sun beating against his dark skin as he idly discussed the interwoven notions of love, sex, and the sacred with family and friends. He was delighted as somebody began playing the drums at a distance as he indulged in another warm grape, smiling with pleasure. It was the summer of love, and he felt safe and passionate.

Meanwhile, across the world in Germany, a young woman sat nervously in a utilitarian doctor's office waiting for the gynecologist's explanation of why her first intercourse had been so excruciatingly painful. As a young child she had enjoyed a sense of freedom in her body while frolicking, often completely nude, in the hot German summers with her nine siblings; that feeling of freedom changed drastically when she entered puberty. Elsbeth had nobody to ask about why her first act of intercourse had hurt so much. Conversations about sex beyond the basics of how babies were made were not at all customary in her household. When she was sixteen, her father had called her a whore for wearing makeup after she returned one evening from a ballroom dance class with her first boyfriend.

The gynecologist interrupted her thoughts with his determination that a small medical procedure was needed to ease Elsbeth's pain, and he completed it that day in the office.

For his part, eight-year-old Freddy's life was changing as he went to live with his dad and new white stepmother while his three siblings stayed with his birth mother after their parents' separation. He always felt loved by his father, a psychiatrist and student of Tantra, and was often surrounded by a supportive and open-minded community of family friends.

One day, Freddy, by now in his mid teens, sat on the home boat in a circle comprised of a blend of Tantric-curious individuals who had attended his father's workshops, as well as friends, colleagues, and his father and stepmother. When a silence briefly passed over the group, Freddy took the opportunity to ask his dad some questions about things that had happened during his recent first sexual experience. His father and some of the group members freely advised and educated him without inhibitions.

Later that day a package was waiting on the dining room table. "Son, I want you to read this," his father said warmly.

Freddy unwrapped his first book about sacred sexuality, and after graciously thanking his father, retreated to his bedroom to read and learn more.

Back in Germany, days after the gynecological procedure, Elsbeth's boyfriend announced his intention to leave the relationship. Heartbroken, she went home, where she found her father sitting at the kitchen table, a letter in his hands, his face livid.

"What have you done?" he shouted, and she realized in that moment the letter was the bill from the gynecologist. Her father now knew what she had been up to. After being subjected to a harsh reprimand, Elsbeth retreated to her bedroom feeling alone and dejected, as if the world had turned against her.

Thirty years later, Elsbeth, residing in Chicago as a US citizen, had become a successful management consultant who traveled the world. One evening while on assignment for a multinational power company in Europe, she went back to her corporate apartment and paused for a moment, resting her head against the inside of the apartment door, keys still in the lock. She shut her eyes and breathed deeply. This moment of reflection brought back the deep despair she felt over a relationship with a married man she could not free herself from. She scanned her apartment, heart heavy. She felt trapped in a cycle of attraction to unavailable men and lacked hope of ever finding fulfillment and sustaining love.

Confronted with the futility of her love situation, she went to a Buddhist meditation retreat at Plum Village in the south of France. Ten days in silent meditation had her face her feelings, actions, and illusions. It was excruciating! Yet those days helped her to connect with her spirit and turn her life around.

In her soul searching, Elsbeth immersed herself in the study of the ancient practice of Tantra that opened her up to her sexual-spiritual self. Deep healing and clearing allowed her to see her unconscious programming around love and intimacy. She came to experience deeper trust in herself and see that she no longer needed to look for love outside—she had discovered love within as a state of being.

To Freddy, Chicago was a new city bustling with possibilities and potential. He had led a life of moving between corporate jobs and relationships with ease during the previous two decades when living in San Francisco. His true passion lay in creative pursuits, but fear of a loss of stability drove him to stay in unfulfilling professional situations and pursue the performing arts only as a hobby. Everything had been shaken up by this move to Chicago looking for newness, diversion, and a new direction for his life. Faced with the opportunity of creating anew, Freddy found room to breathe and to reconnect with his creative self. He grinned, imagining again the standup comedian's stage that had once been so familiar to him from his early days in San Francisco and the Djembe drumming that used to delight his spirit.

A desire for deeper self-expression and authentically sharing his gift brought resolve to bring focus to his life. How to channel creativity and pleasure became a pursuit inspired by his Tantric practice and ongoing learning.

Then he met a woman. He didn't know much about her yet, just what her profile on a Tantric dating website had detailed and what small stories they had traded over a week of e-mail contact. Standing on her doorstep, he composed himself, feeling good about meeting this woman he wanted to know more about.

She had learned from his profile that he had grown up in a Tantric household, an interesting detail that immediately caught her attention and curiosity. Smoothing her hands over her dress once more, she felt a flutter of pleasant anticipation when the doorbell rang.

As Freddy looked up the steps and Elsbeth looked back at him, they sensed that this encounter had the potential for a new future for them. That night they shared wine and food, laughter and conversation, hopes and aspirations, and Tantric connection. Indeed this budding relationship was born of a desire to create love versus unconsciously falling into it and bringing forth a higher purpose together beyond playing out the romantic drama.

This was the beginning of discovering joint purpose and direction in their personal and professional lives. A few months into the relationship, they birthed TantraNova, their transformational company. Integrating sex, love, and consciousness had opened a door to wholeness within each of them and in their relationship. They have come to coin this evolved state of being "sexual enlightenment." How to share this opportunity to heal, transform, and consciously create fulfillment in life and relationships became their mission for years to come.

After leading hundreds of workshops and assisting thousands of couples and singles since that first auspicious rendezvous, Elsbeth and Freddy share with you in this book how you can also enter the world of sexual enlightenment and travel the road of creative joy and sexual, emotional, and spiritual wholeness.

Enjoy the journey!

PART I

Sexual Enlightenment

Chapter 1
What Is Sexual Enlightenment?

*Evolution is evolving from unconscious
chance to conscious choice.*
—Barbara Marx Hubbard, *Birth 2012 and Beyond*

"Sexual enlightenment"? The term isn't well known, nor is it something that has been developed traditionally. In our work, we consider sexual enlightenment to be distinguished by two dimensions. The first involves sexual life-force energy, which brings forth life in all that is alive—human beings, animals, and plants. This energy is at the core of universal consciousness and was around long before we became aware of ourselves, long before the discovery of $E=mc^2$. It's a built-in knowingness given by nature, the Divine, or the eternal consciousness. Sexual life-force energy is the spark of creation that got us here.

The second dimension of sexual enlightenment involves the human capacity to be self-reflective or aware of one's own existence, particularly becoming aware and conscious of one's life-force energy that is sexual in nature, which allows for integrating one's sexual, emotional, and spiritual being. In contrast to animals, who follow their procreative wiring when "in heat," human beings have the potential to bring awareness and consciousness to their sexual selves—their feelings, thoughts, sensations, and behaviors—which can create the opportunity to be at choice regarding the use of their life-force or sexual energy.

Therefore, as reflective humans, we can develop the capacity to bring awareness to the spark of life within us and use this not only in sexual acts but also to create our whole lives—a possibility we explore in further depth in the course of this book. We are particularly interested in bringing to light the manifestation of sexual energy for the sake of conscious and joyous creation of our lives, relationships, careers, and communities.

Thus, sexual enlightenment entails becoming conscious of our life-force sexual energy and tapping into creativity and pleasure—the built-in key aspects of that life-giving spark—as a conduit to greater fulfillment in life and love.

Human Energy

As we learned in our physics and chemistry classes in school, energy can take many forms:

- Electrical energy lights up the sky during thunderstorms and illuminates our homes at night.
- Kinetic energy sends a ball flying through the air when we hit it with a bat.
- Chemical energy drives our bodies' systems and keeps us moving physically.
- Thermal energy can heat our houses and the food we eat.

However, absent from high school and college curriculums is "human energy" as it manifests in our bodies and consciousness. Human life-force energy is sexual in nature (though we are not talking here about traditional sex education) and encompasses a range of states from subtle to intensely aroused. We become aware of this energy when it shows up in procreation, when we are having sex, but it can also be much vaster than—and just as potent—as what we experience during sex. It can be used to create whatever we want to bring into our lives such as good health, well-being, fulfilling relationships, aspirations, and careers.

The sex act is one way of experiencing and using sexual energy but not the only way; intercourse is one stage in the continuum of experiencing sexual energy. Without sexual energy, none of us would be here. It is fundamental not just to human existence but to all of life as we know it and has been present since the very dawn of creation. We will build on this further in chapter 2.

Though we cannot see it, life force sexual energy is ever-present when we are aroused in the bedroom as well as when we are at rest and sex is the furthest thing from our minds—and every state in between. It's even there when we're doing mundane tasks like cooking dinner or getting dressed in the morning.

Sexual energy in its physical manifestation and experience is unique in that it's creative and pleasurable. This allows for the continuing existence of life, which is part of us by nature. We can learn to draw on this awareness of creativity and pleasure, similar to when we're in a loving space or viewing a work of art or in anything we regularly find joy. Our contention is that *when life force sexual energy is unencumbered and free of past personal stories and collective interpretations that no longer serve us, creativity and pleasure are more accessible to us everywhere in life.* It is present where we live, in the people we surround ourselves with, and in the work we do. When we learn sexual consciousness practices, creativity and pleasure start showing up as a default way of being in the simple process of living.

Becoming the Observer

Sexual enlightenment begins when we bring intention and focused attention to our life-force sexual energy. Unlike animals that work simply on biological imperatives to keep their kind from becoming extinct, we have the ability to become the observer of our desires, impulses, wants, fears, and joys. Of course we're wired in that biological dimension as well; in the big picture we're animals ourselves, and it's our inherent mission to continue to thrive generation after generation. In this dimension of sexual energy, we are *machines*—it doesn't require consciousness on our part. It's automatic and just happens whether we're aware of it or not.

What separates us from the beasts, then, is the second dimension of bringing consciousness to sexual energy: our ability to be self-reflective or aware of our own existence, what we call "the observer of the self." This uniquely human capacity allows us to rise above the biological miracle of ourselves and recognize that we are at choice in how we live, feel, and act, including our sexual beingness.

Being "at choice" means we are able to see what is versus what we think should be. This allows us to become clear about what we truly want and take effective action toward fulfilling it. When we are aware of being at choice regarding our sexual beingness, we can tap into and use our sexual energy in a multitude of ways, depending on what we want to create in our lives and relationships. We can use it in the sex act. We can connect with our sacredness and deepen the intimate connection with our beloved. We can integrate our sexual, emotional, and spiritual being. We can use it to fuel our work creatively or connect consciously with the people around us.

Developing this state of mind is essential to working with sexual energy, to tapping in to it and utilizing it to create fulfilling lives. *Without the observer mind, we can be doomed to an eternity of automatic and habitual behaviors that often produce suffering and a sense of being victimized by life.* In other words, we live devoid of creativity and pleasure.

To illustrate the "observer mind," let's look at a moose walking through a forest, just going along her merry way. Then suddenly a big tree falls right in front of her. The moose looks at the tree, lifts her nose to smell it, and then nibbles on the tree's twigs and leaves. As she eats, rain starts to fall. The moose raises her head, enjoying and tasting the drops that fall on her face. When she's had her fill, she simply finds her way around the fallen tree and continues on her journey.

Now say a human is walking through the forest when suddenly a big tree falls right in front of him. He'll look angrily at the tree, cursing and huffing, "Now I'm going to be late for my meeting. And what about my wife and children and my retirement fund? I have to make a bridge to get where I need to go! What? It's raining *too*?" Throwing his hands up in despair and disgust, he'll exclaim, "Why me, God? Why me?"

Becoming like the moose allows us to be in the present moment, witness what is, notice how we feel, and watch the chatter, thoughts, and interpretations in our mind. As humans we are programmed to dwell on the drama that's already passed instead of focusing on the present. Instead of getting caught up in the chatter of the mind, we can cultivate our capacity to be like the moose—simply be with what is happening right here and now. In this witness or observer state, we are connected with ourselves and tap into stillness and peace, and that's the space where intimacy and consequently sexual enlightenment arise.

Getting Enlightened

Sexual enlightenment gives people a glimpse through the doorway to their own power. When people come to our TantraNova workshops, they arrive with wishes, desires, and intentions for things they want to work on, for what they want to change, improve on, or expand into. In the work we do, we have led many to begin to see richer ways to live and coached them to move toward fulfilling their dreams and hopes. This all starts with becoming sexually enlightened through the conscious integration of one's sexual, emotional, and spiritual self.

Moving toward sexual enlightenment requires skill building in three areas:

1. Conscious breathing
2. Meditation – the observer state of mind
3. Energy awareness, both non-aroused and aroused

Conscious Breathing

Breath is the essence of life. From our first moment fresh from the womb until the last sigh of death, we are breathing. Most of the time, we breathe reflexively without thinking, inhaling and exhaling our way through morning routines; work, car, or train rides, exercise, and sleep.

Using breath consciously as a tool is the first step to entering the mindful world of sexual energy. When we are present with our breath, we can reach a place of focus, stillness, and inner peace that allows us to go deeper into ourselves and our experiences. Particularly breathing into the expansion of the abdomen, called the belly breath, allows for activating the parasympathetic or involuntary nervous system. This slows down the heartbeat, relaxes the muscles, and makes us feel good. We drop out of the head and into the body.

Using conscious breathing practices enables us to calm the incessant chatter of the mind and become witnesses to our thoughts, feelings, and sensations. When we are in this place of observing ourselves, we stop being stuck in our feelings, desires, and automatic wiring and instead witness *what's running us*.

Meditation

Calming the chatter in the mind is at the core of bringing focus and attention to sexual energy. If we cannot be present with ourselves, how can we be present with one another?

Many meditation practices lead to the same intended outcome: *being able to be present and at peace with what is.* These practices can be active, passive, social, or sexual in nature. Sexual meditation is powerful because it helps us become physically, chemically, emotionally, and spiritually connected, loving, and vulnerable. It can show up in various manifestations in the body, heart, and mind:

> Physically: your heart rate increases; you feel more sensitive and aware; you may have a warm, supple sensation.

> Chemically: oxytocin and endorphins are enhanced, resulting in deeper relaxation and calmness and decreased pain or discomfort.

Emotionally: you feel more content, open, receptive, joyous, and trusting.

Spiritually: you experience a sense of being connected with yourself and the universe.

Sexual meditation is probably the most difficult form of meditation to master because we are so used to getting completely swept up in the excitement and drama of sex. Nothing is wrong with excitement and drama, yet to become sexually enlightened you want to learn how to move beyond them and become conscious of non-aroused and aroused energy. Doing this requires willingness and practice.

Meditation allows for a magnified accessibility to what may unconsciously run us so we can become aware, be at choice, and shift what we want to shift in ourselves and our relationships. *We can become more aware of where we are regarding sexual energy as it relates to fear, guilt, embarrassment, and shame—all the factors that often weigh us down and keep us from attaining what we want in life.* When we can consciously access our sexual energy, we can transform these blocks or constrictions and move toward fuller expression of ourselves.

Energy Awareness

Sexual energy as a conscious source of creativity and pleasure is only available once we engage in becoming aware of and attuned to life-force energy running through our physical bodies at all times, like a current through a wire. When we can bring awareness to that flow, we can start channeling it. This is not rocket science, but it requires focused practice that will lead to being able to channel aroused sexual energy at a more advanced state, bringing greater consciousness to oneself and deeper fulfillment to one's relationships.

Just as the yoga we primarily practice in the West focuses on the physical body, Tantra yoga and the TantraNova approach focus on the energetic body. To distinguish the energetic body we draw on energy fields based in the system of the chakras (see chapter 5 for further explanation) and the interconnected flow of energy up and down the spine (also called *Kundalini* in Sanskrit).

One important step in the process of moving toward a state of sexual enlightenment is the integration of these energy fields, which results in a sense of wholeness. When we are in a state of integration, we don't experience any blocks or constrictions in the energy flow within our body. Life-force energy can move freely from one center to another, keeping us in balance in body, heart, and mind. In this state we are at peace and so better able not just to live fulfilling lives but really to discover—or uncover— who we are.

Chapter 2
Sexual Energy

Fortunate, indeed, is the person who has discovered to give sex emotion an outlet through some form of creative effort, for he has, by that discovery, lifted himself to the status of a genius.
—Napoleon Hill, *Think and Grow Rich*

In his 1937 classic *Think and Grow Rich*, Napoleon Hill identified a number of principles of success for those who are inclined to study and practice. One of these principles he called "sex transmutation," by which he meant the changing or transferring of one form of energy into another form. According to Hill, sexual desire may be the most powerful human desire that can be "transmuted" with imagination, willpower, and persistence into creative endeavors such as art, business, and the accumulation of wealth. His insights were particularly forward thinking at the time when he wrote his book, which focused on business leaders and what makes them successful.

Just like Hill, we consider sexual life-force energy to be the spark of life in all of its expression. Sexual energy and life-force energy are one and the same. This energy is an undercurrent that has always existed; it is part of the universal intelligence that has been present forever and everywhere. It is joy and pleasure; it is creativity.

Life-force energy is the fuel for creating life in many forms, from procreation to building and sustaining relationships, to running a business or even decorating our home. It's transparent—most of the time we're not aware of it—but it's always there. We may feel sexual energy in sensations and emotions that don't appear to be sexual; we may feel it in just the simple pleasure of existing. Sexual energy is the spark that's creating life as we know it.

When we bring conscious awareness to our sexual energy—a capacity that is unique to human beings—we can use it to turbo charge the integration of our physical, emotional, and spiritual selves. This in turn allows for more fulfilling lives with expanded creativity, joy, and pleasure and for more fulfilling relationships with our significant others, our friends, our families, our business partners, our communities, and finally the world as a whole.

Freeing Sexual Life-Force Energy

Lisa was an accomplished international management consultant. Curiosity brought her to TantraNova, which—as it turned out later—was the beginning of a turning point in her life. Her career was a major focus for her, and continuing education in formal and informal settings had become part of her life. While she considered herself successful as indicated by external measures, she knew something was not fully expressed in herself and her work, yet she was unable to pinpoint what was missing.

Lisa's journey at TantraNova assisted her in becoming aware of her energetic body, her proneness to automatic emotional reactions, and the rampant conversations and interpretations that preoccupied her mind. While she had sharpened her intellect through her academic work and had become more aware of her emotional self through a coaching program she attended, it was not until she experienced a freeing of her life-force energy in sexual and intimate ways that she was able to clear old stories and imprints from childhood and adolescence. Freeing herself from some expectation of who she was supposed to be to embracing her unique gifts and authentic self opened the door to reconnect with her aliveness in a whole new way. As a result of setting free her creative self, she began to reinvent who she was in the world. She left her corporate career and went on to found a transformational-leadership center.

Universal Consciousness and Sexual Energy

When we say "universal consciousness," we speak of the ever-present force that exists—and has always existed—within and around us throughout the infinite universe. Sexual energy is a manifestation of universal consciousness that has been creating, sustaining, and expanding life for billions of years. Evolved from single-celled amoebae to multicell organisms, we have become aware of this creative universal intelligence as a life-giving aspect of our biological existence as well as the fuel and foundation for living a creative, fulfilled, and inspired life. Developing a listening for this creative universal intelligence in terms of sexual life-force energy is at the core of sexual enlightenment. This allows us to deliberately acquire new awareness and behaviors to create satisfying lives.

The state of our awareness of sexual life-force energy at this time in the process of human evolution can be compared to the state of the world prior to Einstein's theory of relativity. Before his discovery, relativity was a principle by which the universe had been operating all along, yet we were not able to recognize it. Einstein opened a door to a new understanding that altered science and the way of life for the human race. Practical applications of relativity theory include the capacity to produce nuclear energy, alleviating a portion of our reliance on nonrenewable resources for our energy needs; synchronizing global positioning system (GPS) satellites around the earth; or acknowledging philosophically that there is no universal truth, only a relative truth based on a person's or community's perception of the world.

Bringing light to the principle of sexual life-force energy the way Einstein brought awareness to the principle of relativity is our intention. The shift in awareness holds the possibility of altering the way we feel about ourselves, the way we create our lives, and the way we relate to and coordinate effectively with others in our intimate, familial, and professional relationships.

Sexual Energy in History

Throughout the ages, sexual energy has been described—and experienced—in many different ways by many different peoples. Pockets of understanding arose in various cultures at certain points of their development, but for one reason or another they died down again.

For example, ancient Hindus practiced sexual rites as part of their Tantric tradition not only as a means of physical arousal but to bring attunement and harmony to themselves and their relationships and facilitate heightened states of awareness. This was a highly spiritual endeavor that brought about an experience of spiritual-sexual oneness and connectedness. Tapping into the universal intelligence in this way and setting creative life-force energy free allowed for an inspired and powerful state of being in life and relationships.

Using meditation, conscious breathing, and channeling energy to prolong and enhance orgasmic joy by oneself or with a partner is one level of experiencing that sexual life-force energy. While this was an aspect of the original Hindu rite, it was not the sole purpose; physical arousal and pleasure were merely enjoyable offshoots of the overall connection with oneself and the universe. This is one of the main tenets of our TantraNova teachings: to learn to sustain and consciously circulate precious life-force energy for the man so he may become more balanced in his masculine and feminine nature; and to reawaken luscious feminine energy for the woman so she may let go into receiving and trusting while connecting with her feminine essence. For each, these attainments will help achieve aliveness and well-being within, in partnership, and in the way we approach life. The practices lead not only to enhancing your experience in the bedroom but to creating fulfillment in your relationships, career, hobbies, or anything else you have a desire to bring about in your life.

Another example of the origins of the quest to discover and bring conscious awareness to our sexual energy leads us to the ancient Taoists in China thousands of years ago. The Taoists believed performing "the bedroom arts," as they called them, could help one to stay in good health and increase longevity. As far back as the Han Dynasty, some Taoist secrets referred to intercourse as "joining energy" and treated it as a sacred, spiritual practice. They believed conscious lovemaking allowed for harnessing sexual energy in order to replenish life force. At one time this was a well-known and often-discussed topic in Chinese society. However, as Confucianism became more prominent, Puritanism took hold of the culture, and the bedroom arts disappeared from public life.

Sexual life-force energy has been considered magical from the beginning of time given that it creates life. Creativity and pleasure are inherent in this energy, and when we are tapped into this energy we experience life creatively and pleasurably, like *things are working.* As big-brain thinking Homo sapiens, we are now able to use our conscious mind to focus and draw on this energy and allow creativity and pleasure to show up in areas of life that seem completely unrelated to sex.

The Science of Sexual Energy

Energy is ever-present in all that is alive as well as all that is inert. In essence, everything is energy manifesting in different forms at different times. For example, energy can manifest as physical matter such as the floor beneath the chair on which you sit. Or it can be a liquid such as the water in your drinking glass, or even a gas such as the air you breathe. It all depends on the density and frequency of the energy.

Underlying all the seemingly separate objects and forms of matter is an undercurrent that is identified in physics as "string theory." This states that all matter, physical and nonphysical, is connected. This principle, which exists on the subatomic level, is replete through the cosmos ad infinitum. String theory encompasses Einstein's theory of relativity and is generally believed—even by some of the greatest thinkers of our time, including Stephen Hawking—to be a *theory of everything.* In other words, through the lens of string theory we can describe all fundamental forces and matter in the universe.

According to string theory, everything—my body, the table at which I sit, the air I breathe, the person I work with—is interconnected by oscillating threads called "string vibrations." Of course this flies in the face of the more traditional Newtonian and Cartesian thinking, which are mechanistic and component-based. In Sir Isaac Newton's and René Descartes's views, the world was to be understood—from the human body down to a blade of grass—by taking it apart into its components.

In contrast, string theory says everything and everyone is connected rather than separate, whether it's the system of your body, your relationships, your family, all citizens in the country in which you live, or the people of the entire planet Earth. While there is a demarcation between your physical body and someone else's, the viewpoint of string theory shows our interrelatedness and connection energetically, which implies that we and all the other people and things in our lives influence one another whether for good or bad. In a practical way, this view allows us to see ourselves in each other.

Application of Energy

Unless it takes the form of light—as in sunlight or a lightbulb—we are not able to see energy with the naked eye. While we can hear acoustic energy via our eardrums or sense thermal energy via our skin, we cannot see the frequencies that make it happen. To visually demonstrate this elusive circuit of energy within oneself and then between two or more people, we use what we call an "energy ball" at our TantraNova workshops. It's basically a plastic ball that operates on an open/closed system. Freddy Zental first demonstrates this circuit within himself by holding the ball with both hands and touching the metal pads on opposing sides of it with his index fingers. The electrical circuit within him is completed, and the ball lights up. When he removes one finger, the ball turns dark.

Next, Freddy Zental holds the ball in his left hand with his index finger on one of the ball's metal pads while Elsbeth puts her right index finger on the other metal pad. Then Elsbeth places her left hand in Freddy Zental's right hand, and, to many workshop participants' surprise, the ball lights up once again. This is because the circuit between the two is closed—they are energetically connected.

After that they add in the workshop participants—anywhere from ten to sixty at a time—until a large circle is formed. They all hold hands, creating a long circuit ending with Freddy Zental and Elsbeth—and the energy ball between them. With their fingers on the metal plates, and everyone in the circle joined, the circuit becomes closed, and the ball is lit. When one of the participants separates his or her hand from a neighbor's hand, the ball goes dark.

This might sound simple, but it can be a powerful demonstration for someone who has never considered how energetically interconnected we all are. It can further reveal how our thoughts, emotions, and actions might affect our relationships with our partners, children, coworkers, and friends. This demonstration with the energy ball gives our workshop participants a sense that something exists beyond what we can see. It makes energy visible.

Most people are not aware of energy that exists both within and around them—unless it comes to them in the form of a bolt of lightning or a lightbulb sparking to life. And in our culture, we have been trained to believe that if we can't see it, it doesn't exist. The solution then is to start becoming aware of that energetic dimension of our human existence and of the frequencies that tie all of us together.

One of our goals is to turn on that light.

Chapter 3
Life Force and the Conscious Mind

There is a vitality, a life force, an energy, a quickening, that
is translated through you into action, and because there is
only one of you in all time, this expression is unique.
—Martha Graham, Modern Dancer and Choreographer

Life-force energy brings forth life. Its purpose is self-evident. It makes sense then that it will be present only in forms that themselves contain life and are fueled by that innate energy. There is no life-force or sexual energy in inert states such as gases, or in non-living objects such as rocks.

First and foremost, the purpose of life force or sexual energy is to perpetuate the existence of human, animal, and plant life. Procreation is the action we use to continue life on this planet. Without life-force energy, none of us would be here. There would be no spark of life, no drive to procreate—which, as we discussed in chapter 2, is an innate urge in all living beings, including animals and plants. Procreation is the basis of life; it is the primal means of our own propagation, a total expression of what life-force energy is all about.

However, there is also a difference between humans and animals, as we alluded to in chapter 1. As human beings, we are linguistic in nature—meaning we have the capacity of making promises, declaring who we are being or becoming, assessing the past, and distinguishing interpretations from facts (see speech act theory as developed by John Langshaw Austin and John Rogers Searle in the 1950s and '60s respectively and made further accessible—beyond academia—to business and organizational environments by Fernando Flores in the 1980s).

This linguistic capacity allows us to be self-reflective and aware of our own existence. This implies that we can bring conscious awareness to our life-force sexual energy, whereas other animals cannot. Let's say a bull and a cow are in heat and move through the mating process. Upon completion, the bull won't turn to the cow and say, "Dear, that was exceptionally great sex."

Similarly for humans, making a baby can be done unconsciously; it's part of our wiring. In animals we call this "going into heat," which happens based on biological and environmental factors such as the seasons of the year. In this way humans are similar to animals—our urge to reproduce is largely biological, and it's something that can happen whether we are aware of it or not. Women's bodies have built-in ovulation and menstrual cycles that tell them, albeit subconsciously, when it is time to have sex in order to create a baby. In turn, women and men are said to emit pheromones, chemicals that trigger our sense of smell and attract us to the opposite sex when the time for mating is ideal.

However, life-force energy is not *solely* about procreation. In fact, it is far more than that. When we are in an aroused state of our life-force sexual energy, we experience joy, pleasure, and intimacy with ourselves and/or with another. These emotions and sensations arise from increased hormonal flow as bodily manifestations of the activity. Unlike animals, humans are blessed with being able to experience pleasure for pleasure's sake without necessarily having to procreate. Self-reflection allows us to bring forth our experiences by using our conscious minds. If we wish, we can use life-force energy in a conscious way beyond the realm of procreation, for other purposes such as fueling our creative self, enhancing our physical health, embellishing our love relationships, and consciously creating our lives.

Manifestations of Life-force energy

As a force of nature, life-force energy has been around since the dawn of creation. In history it has been distinguished by many cultures and in many areas of the world: in the Chinese tradition it is called *chi*; in Sanskrit, *Kundalini*; in Vedantic philosophy, *prana*; in Hawaiian culture, *mana*; in Tibetan Buddhism, *Lüng*; in the Japanese culture, *Reiki*; in Western philosophy, *vital energy*; and in modern pop culture, The Force (as in *Star Wars*). Westerners today may be familiar with some of these terms from their use in practices such as tai chi, qigong, Reiki sessions, or Kundalini yoga.

No matter what it has been called, life-force energy has always existed as a constant in the universe and within us, fueling our bodies and keeping us alive from one moment to the next. If we stopped breathing, we would die. It is life-force energy or prana (energetic breath) that, on a very basic level, keeps our bodies performing the parasympathetic or unconscious functions we need to survive. When we become conscious of our breath and aware of life-force energy running through us all the time, we can begin to channel that energy into larger, more-refined purposes such as creating or appreciating art, vitalizing physical health, finding passion in our work, and experiencing lasting and meaningful love.

Before we get into how to achieve such awareness and results, let's take a look at the three ways in which life-force energy can manifest in the human being: the physical body, the emotional body, and the mental body.

The Physical Body: Pleasure and Pain

Energy in the physical body is experienced in terms of sensations. We can think of the nervous system as an electrical grid that's equipped with sensors. Sensations may range from severe pain to extreme pleasure and everything in between. For example, when we engage sexually, we usually feel pleasure (or at least that is the ultimate goal toward which we strive). I touch my body, or someone else touches me, and the pressure on my flesh or the friction on my skin triggers a physical response or sensation I experience as pleasure—my skin feels tingly, my breathing rate increases, my pulse quickens, my face feels hot, and so on.

Sensations may also be experienced in other ways. When we're sad we may feel tightness in our chest or constriction in the throat. When we are angry we may feel a knot in the solar plexus or have an upset stomach. Joy may be felt throughout the body or specifically around the heart center. These somatic reactions are correlated to feelings and emotions we may have or thoughts and interpretations that got triggered.

The Emotional Body: Our Feelings

Energy in the emotional body is experienced in terms of feelings and emotions such as anger, resentment, regret, love, joy, and peace. For example, when you lose someone you love, you feel grief. When something does not go the way you anticipated it would, you might feel anger or frustration. When things go your way, a feeling of contentment may result.

Feelings and emotions are brought on by triggers either from the outside or by a thought or memory. Think about a flash of anger, a surge of happiness, and so many other sayings that speak to the immediate, sometimes startling nature of our emotions. They often come unbidden and unplanned, taking our bodies and minds by surprise.

Our emotional and physical bodies are intrinsically linked. For each emotion there is a somatic response. The human being is a great and intricate machine composed of many interlocking and interdependent systems. It should be no shock then that our emotions should affect our bodies as well as the other way around.

The Mental Body: Interpretations and Stories

Energy in the mental body manifests in terms of thoughts, interpretations, or stories that may be triggered by external circumstances or internal conversations. We are automatically prone to assigning meaning to people, things, and events in our lives. For example, a car on the highway has pulled out in front of yours, causing you to slow down. One possibility is that this is simply an action that has no inherent meaning and therefore no ensuing emotion or sensation as a consequence. The simple fact is this car is now in front of yours—end of story.

However, as humans, we are more like wired trigger bombs, reacting to things that push our buttons, setting us off, so to speak. Here the trigger is the car pulling out in front of you, a neutral act until the automatic interpretation sets in, which takes only a nanosecond. This could play out in the following way: The other driver has cut you off on purpose, and anger flares in your body, quickening your pulse and making your blood pressure rise. In other words, due to your mind's interpretation, your emotional and physical body have been spurred on to reaction.

You can continue to feel angry and disturbed and victimized, which might lead you to put your foot on the gas and tailgate the other driver while giving him the finger and the high beams. Or you can make a conscious decision to shift out of this auto-emotional state of reaction and actually invent other interpretations by calling on your "witness state." For example, you can instead think the other driver simply didn't see your car, or maybe he's in a hurry to get his wife, who is pregnant and in labor, to the nearest hospital. He might have a good reason for his driving—one you literally know nothing about. With this in mind, you can calm yourself down, bring your pulse and your blood pressure back to normal levels, and continue driving in a safe and responsible manner with inner peace.

Realistically, how often do we consider taking that second path? We'd bet not often. It's in our nature to react with anger when we feel someone has done us wrong. For example, when you were two, perhaps you didn't get the exact toy you wanted for Christmas, and in your experience at the time you felt you were no longer loved. For you that meant there was something wrong with you, because why wouldn't your parents have given you exactly what you asked for?

To cope with that excruciating feeling, you busied yourself with playing and breaking your siblings' new toys, reacting with revenge. From that moment on, the response became coded within your nervous system, in essence hardwiring itself into your body's makeup. Now you—and most of the rest of us—are programmed to react with anger or revenge when you feel like you don't get what you asked for, because to you that means you are not loved.

The Choice

With training we can become aware of these various manifestations of energy in terms of sensations, emotions, or interpretations and can start rewiring ourselves. We can learn to notice and witness triggers from our *observer state of mind* and can retrace a familiar feeling, thought, or physical reaction to an earlier incident in life. By "un-collapsing" past experiences from present ones, we can leave the past in the past where it belongs and live our lives more fully in the here and now.

At TantraNova we have created a particular practice that we named "Recall," which entails the un-collapsing of present experiences from the past via a guided process particularly as they relate to love, sex, and intimacy. Participants connect with and articulate their uniquely personal stories through accessing feelings, sensations, and underlying interpretations. They then rewrite those stories according to how they would have wanted the past experiences to have gone and create and express new stories interactively with others in the workshop. The latter allows for a cellular shift in the nervous system that, in turn, alters a person's physical, emotional, and mental body.

This practice assists in developing the capacity to free oneself from feeling the victim of circumstances and shift out of a reactive way of being. Now we can choose how we want to feel and experience life and how to encounter what's happening in our lives and relationships.

PART II

A Call to Awareness

Chapter 4
The Three Key Dimensions

And no one will listen to us until we listen to ourselves.
—Marianne Williamson, *A Return to Love*

How can we become more aware of and attuned to life force, this flow of energy ever moving through us? Here are distinctions that provide us with guideposts and will orient us on our journey in terms of energy awareness.

The human body contains seven major energy centers known as *chakras*. The ancient masters of the Eastern traditions of China and India described the chakras as a system of energy fields; chakra is a Sanskrit word that refers to wheels of light that vibrate at particular frequencies measurable in hertz—a truly scientific phenomenon that occurs within our bodies whether we choose to recognize it or not.

Each chakra is associated with an area of the body and the functions that area controls. For example, the throat chakra correlates to our vocal chords, ears, and throat and affects our abilities to communicate and listen. The crown chakra, located on the top of the head, is related to the brain and pituitary gland and deals with the connection to our higher or spiritual self.

These chakras, or energy centers, can be thought of as energy fields with center-specific frequencies through which our emotional, mental, and spiritual worlds interact with the physical world within and around us. For example, when someone you love dies, even years later you can think about that person and feel something—sad, mad, upset, whatever it may be. And you can feel those emotions in your body: sadness in your chest or the heart chakra; anger in the pit of your stomach or the power chakra; speechlessness in the throat chakra; or confusion in the mind, the location of the third-eye chakra.

We consider these feelings and sensations indicators of our energetic body, which is just as real for each of us as our physical body, yet we have learned to disregard or dismiss our emotions and rationalize ourselves out of sensing what goes on within us. When something happens that we experience as an interruption or interference, such as the painful ending of a relationship or the loss of a job, we say things such as "I have to let it go," or "I have to get over it and get on with my life," and many other phrases that push aside and willfully ignore the very concerns that might activate blocks in our energy centers. This in turn has us experiencing disconnects in our outer lives such as problems in relationships, dissatisfaction with our jobs, or even physical illnesses that can, at times, be serious in nature.

This *avoidance of feeling what we feel*, particularly when those feelings are unpleasant, can produce suppression on the emotional level, tightness on the somatic level, and mental blocks on the intellectual level. The avoidance makes us stagnate, leaving us stuck in a state of unrest and unease, even paralyzed at times; it also keeps us from living life fully and joyously.

Many people, when arriving at such a crossroads, do not know how to handle it. Traditionally we have not been taught how to handle the emotions we naturally experience on a day-to-day basis, much less the sometimes-overwhelming emotions that accompany major life events. We learn that feelings must be controlled at all costs, and if we have any emotions we find confusing or difficult to parse, we may feel shame or embarrassment. Or we are trained early on to keep them to ourselves so as not to make others uncomfortable by forcing them to deal with our less-than-pretty feelings. In this way we can become so unfamiliar with interacting with our own emotions that we are afraid of sharing our intimate selves—and in time we can become unable to do so even if we find we might want to.

Thus stifled, many people find their only outlets in addiction, turning to drugs, alcohol, gambling, dangerous sex, or whatever they feel may bring temporary relief. However, the use of behaviors or substances to avoid unpleasant feelings and sensations can only further promote this disconnect from oneself. Becoming willing to go toward the discomfort allows us to get to the other side—to create more happiness and peace within our lives.

When we do bring awareness to our feelings—particularly through conscious breathing and certain energy-awareness practices, as we will examine in chapter 10—we develop the ability to sense energy in terms of physical manifestations: tightness in the chest or heavy breathing; in terms of emotions: grief or sadness; or in terms of interpretations: "there is something wrong with me" or "nobody loves me." Once we can identify these phenomena through conscious listening aided by conscious breathing and the observer state of mind, we can begin to clear any constrictions on the physical, emotional, and intellectual levels. Tuning in to our energetic body and becoming aware of the life-force energy running through us all the time assists us in clearing or removing blocks in terms of physical ailments, emotional suffering, or long-held debilitating or destructive thoughts.

Developing the capacity to affect energy flow in the body is at the core of becoming a more integrated and whole human being physically, emotionally, and spiritually. Life-force or subtle sexual energy runs a constant circuit through the body, emanating from the base of the spine, moving up along the spine to the crown of the head, and then circulating back to the base of the spine. This happens whether we bring awareness to the process or not. If we suffer blocks in any of our energy centers, this flow is disrupted; once an opening, energetically speaking, and a clearing of constrictions has occurred in any of the energy centers, life-force energy can again circulate in an unencumbered way along this path.

If you have ever watched an infant, you have seen this unencumbered flow in the child's physical and emotional being: the movements are fluid, the spine is nimble, and there is no getting stuck in one emotion. The infant moves easily from one emotional state to another—for example, crying when she is hungry, smiling when you play with her, and then gazing peacefully at a mobile. In adults we call this reestablishment of the unencumbered flow a "recalibration of the self," through which we can tap into our life force as an ever-present source and utilize it to create greater well-being, joy, creativity, and pleasure in our physical bodies, lives, and relationships.

Traditional Tantra and Taoism offer insights and practices that lead us to become aware of our life-force energy in daily life as well as in the bedroom. In TantraNova we use the same holistic approach. Bringing awareness or consciousness to that effervescent energy allows us to affect its flow through our bodies at all times, not just when we are at a heightened state of sexual arousal but in everyday, non-aroused situations.

In our approach to evolving the physical, emotional, and spiritual self along the continuum of sexual enlightenment, we focus—in the context of this book—on three of our bodies' chakras or energy centers in particular: the sexual center (the second energy center located right above the pubic bone); the love center (the fourth energy center located in the middle of the chest); and the consciousness center (the sixth energy center located in the middle of the forehead). We call them the "three key dimensions," and while we do not disregard the remaining four energy centers, we feel these three are the most essential to start with in our mission of assisting the people we work with to move toward sexual enlightenment in order to fulfill their dreams and find richer ways to live.

In the context of cultivating sexual enlightenment, the sex, love, and consciousness centers play a key role in shifting the collective and individual unconsciousness as it relates to sex, love, and intimacy. Over the next three chapters, we will examine each of these chakras in depth and explore what they mean in the context of the sexual enlightenment process.

Chapter 5

Sex

Since sexual energy is what creates all life, all life weaves back to it.
—Misha Davenport, *Chicago Sun-Times*

The sexual center is the second chakra in the body, located just above the pubic bone. This center is considered the seat of creativity, aliveness, joy, and pleasure; it is also the area from which new life is conceived and born. This is understandably a powerful center, with the ability to bring forth life itself through procreation, the ultimate creative act in the human existence. This center also sources and influences our lives in terms of creating ourselves and cocreating with others.

When we speak of sex, as we have before, we use the word as simple shorthand to refer to a complex set of physical sensations, emotions, and mental and spiritual connections that embody our experience with the sex act with a partner or with oneself. Truly when we speak about sex, it is not just sex; it is sexual energy, life-force energy, creativity, joy, pleasure, and a means through which we can further our journey toward greater integration, wholeness, and thus sexual enlightenment. By bringing consciousness to our sexual self, we gain greater awareness of how to use and channel life-force energy—in subtle and aroused states—to affect our sexual and pleasure experiences, our relationships, and our lives at large.

However, for us to access our life-force energy as a source and guide to create our lives, most of us need to clear notions of ourselves that—be they of collective or individual heritage—we have been holding from infancy, childhood, or adolescence. When the sexual center is cleared energetically and the static is removed, sexual life-force energy is set free and we can experience ourselves as the source of our experience in the bedroom as well as in any other area of our lives. Shifting out of reactivity to our sexual self and becoming conscious in this way makes us the captain of our ship. This allows us to gain a greater appreciation for the physical wants and desires we experience and acknowledge the life-giving and arousing energy that can have us, or we can have it.

Bringing consciousness to sexual energy enables us to channel and transmute this energy in and outside of the bedroom. In this light we expand on the interpretation of sex, focusing on creativity, joy, and pleasure as a result of consciously connecting with our sexual life-force energy whether it shows up in the act of lovemaking or in the activities of our everyday lives.

Clearing the Blocks

If the flow of energy is impeded by energetic constrictions or blocks, or when the frequency is off, so to speak, within a center or among the centers, energy cannot travel as it is meant to, and we can find ourselves experiencing pain, numbness, or discomfort. We may feel out of balance emotionally, physically, or mentally and unable to experience a sense of wholeness and access sexual enlightenment that will allow us to live a more joyful and creative life.

Over millennia, the collective consciousness—as found in societal norms such as laws, folkloric perspectives, or religious dogma and beliefs—has placed stigmas on the sexual act and anything sexual, from Victorian chastity belts and anti-masturbation devices for preventing nocturnal emission for males to tales of babies being brought by storks to considering sex before marriage a sin to current-day political wars over female reproductive rights.

Where do these attitudes originate? Many cultures have a long, ingrown fear of pleasure and all it entails, and at some stage in our lives, most of us have experienced our sexual being as a source of guilt, fear, shame, or embarrassment. Perhaps it was a parent walking in on you as teenager while you were masturbating in your bedroom, or being slapped on the hand as an infant when touching your genitals; maybe someone told you that enjoying sex was wrong and sinful, or you were sexually abused as a child. It could even have been something such as your parents shouting at you to get out when you, just a child, innocently found them making love in the middle of the night when you should have been in bed. Such a discovery may have taught you that the sex act is a secret, shameful thing to be performed only under cover of darkness, and if you are found out the appropriate reaction is anger.

Many of us have skewed views on sex and sexual expression based on what our parents and society taught us either directly or inadvertently, our connections to anything sexual, and our associated emotions. Our interpretations of both become set in our minds and bodies early on in life. We have found in our work at TantraNova that these memories are often stored on the cellular level in the sexual center, which is therefore deeply connected to these fundamental stories as we have appropriated them into our thinking and experiencing over time.

These stories run our present-day lives and behaviors and the interpretations we have of ourselves and others, although we may be unaware of the extent to which they run us or even of the stories themselves. We may remember some of the events but are not able to see the interconnectedness of past experiences with present-day thoughts, feelings, and actions. For example, we may remember seeing our parents on that one late night, but often we do not realize—because no one has ever assisted us in deciphering the experience—just how deeply it affected us.

Bringing consciousness to these stories around our sexual self and working toward a state of sexual enlightenment requires a willingness to clear out the sexual center of the static in terms of emotions and interpretations that may no longer serve us. Energetically speaking, if these unpleasant emotions and interpretations are not cleared, one may remain emotionally, spiritually, and physically in a state that is absent of ease and lasting joy.

Whenever there is constriction in the sexual life-force center, the flow within the body is inhibited, including life-force energy itself that emanates from the base of the spine. Blood flow may be impeded; breathing may become habitually more shallow; and electrical impulses in the nervous system may be interrupted, resulting in events such as being frozen in shock or at a loss for words. If sexual life-force energy cannot flow freely through the body's energy system, we cannot experience a sense of well-being and, ultimately, sexual enlightenment expressed in greater joy, creativity, and passion in life.

Unencumbered flow within the body is the foundation of one's ability to feel well and healthy physically, emotionally, and spiritually. When our blood flows well, we feel alive; when our emotions flow freely, we feel loved and able to love; when our spiritual senses flow, we feel connected to all of life and indeed to the universe. Connecting consciously with our sexual center through learned practices, as we will lay out in chapter 10, can allow us to clear any blocks that may impede the flow within our bodies and beings in order to access and make use of the life-giving and pleasurable energy that lies therein.

Beyond Sex

Sexual life-force energy—as we mentioned before—is creative and pleasurable in nature. The physical pleasure we can derive from the act of having sex with a partner or with ourselves is a manifestation of sexual life-force energy for us in our physical bodies.

However, having sex is not the only way to access this form of pleasure and utilize it to enhance our lives. Just as pleasure may be experienced as a rush of blood through the torso or the warmth of friction caused by touching a beloved's body during intimate moments, it may also manifest in subtle, nonsexual experiences such as feeling a warm breeze on one's skin, enjoying watching a child building a sand castle, or seeing the sun setting over the horizon.

The key lies in developing our abilities to listen to, notice, and sense how the energy shows up in our body, our emotions, and our interpretive self. Creativity and pleasure are integral and systemic to sexual life-force energy. By developing conscious awareness and learning to access our life-force energy through focused practice, we become more able to experience creativity and pleasure seamlessly in all areas of our life on physical, emotional, mental, and spiritual levels.

Taking off the Blinders

Caterina and her husband had been in a happy and supportive marriage for twenty-five years. Both were fully committed to their partnership, yet Caterina was yearning for a more intimate and sexual connection. When she arrived at TantraNova, she immediately felt at home in the environment. She began to share some things about herself and the sexual incompatibility she experienced with her husband—a concern that had been festering for years. Caterina is a vivacious, sensuous, and outgoing woman with a healthy libido, while her husband's desire for sexual engagement had waned to a zero point of interest. Elevated blood sugars, waning testosterone from age, and a head injury early in his life may have contributed to his lack of sexual desire.

Caterina had reached a breaking point of hopelessness and sadness over her situation. She felt unwanted and unattractive and had completely given up on ever having sex with another. Not only was she not having the amount of sex she wanted, leading to physical and emotional frustration, but the deeper concern was that she equated not having sex with her own worthiness as a woman and as a person. Her husband's not being available for sex meant she was somehow not deserving of love, passion, and happiness in her life.

Through particular TantraNova practices designed to listen to and experience more keenly one's sexual and heart center,

Caterina and her husband came to a new and deeper sense of intimacy that had been totally unexpected before starting the practices, which brought greater consciousness to their marriage and sexual relationship. They acknowledged their authentic truths to one another as they related to their sexual relationship— what they wanted and did not want; their hidden assessments of themselves and each other; and their feelings around unfulfilled dreams. The unmasked truth was difficult to face initially, like pouring salt on an open wound. Yet once it was spoken with clarity, a new space opened between the couple for dialogue and honesty that completely transformed their relationship. They came to experience peace with what was so for them and could reframe their loving relationship, find even deeper love for one another, and welcome new possibilities of self-expression.

Once Caterina started to uncouple her worthiness from sexual attention, she came to realize that she did not have to depend on anyone outside of herself for the love and sense of worthiness she desired. She remembered herself as already being loved and connected with the beloved within while she got to acknowledge the vibrant sexual being she was. We say "remembered" because really she was merely uncovering something that had been true about herself all along; the feelings and stories appropriated and so familiar from early childhood and adolescence and stored energetically in her sexual center (the second chakra) and heart center (the fourth chakra) had made her forget about her magnificent self. Caterina said at the time that it felt as though she were "taking off the blinders" and could now see very clearly what was true for her.

"The truth is," she said, "I no longer need to see my husband as the sole provider responsible for sexual pleasure in my life. Instead I now find that my pleasure originates from within me. It is not something my husband bestowed upon me or owes me."

When Caterina was able to bring conscious awareness to her emotions, sexual desires, and old stories, she reported that her husband's low sex drive became a nonissue. By accessing her sexual life force as a source and resource within herself, she made new discoveries of her sexual, emotional, and spiritual being. Getting that she was an integrated and whole self allowed Caterina to no longer look for sexual fulfillment outside. As the source of her sexual pleasure and love shifted for her, she became free to create passion and happiness for herself and in her relationship with her husband.

"I no longer feel unworthy or unattractive," she said. "I feel free to play and engage in all the great aspects of my relationship with him without the upset from feeling he isn't providing something important that he knows I want."

Caterina reports that she has experienced a new sense of being comfortable in her own skin. She does daily practices that keep her in touch with her life-force energy and has created a stronger sense of self. This has led to a reprioritization of what she wants from her relationship with her husband and a realization that she does not need to be so focused on sex to feel intimacy. Through more frequent affectionate acts such as kissing, cuddling, and the TantraNova heart-to-heart connection practice (see chapter 10) paired with more open communication, Caterina now feels a deeper connection to her husband and says they are experiencing more intimacy than ever before. They are even creating a new workshop business together, which never would have happened with the anger Caterina previously felt. The relationship is blossoming in amazing and unexpected new ways.

In addition—and as often happens when people start to tap in to the flow of life-force energy within—Caterina began to prosper in other ways. Her personality has become lighter and more playful; she has a lot more fun in everything she does; and people seem to be magnetically attracted to her. As a result, her coaching and training business has grown, and her clients experience greater results from her services. She is more able to connect with others through compassion and a self-confidence that grants her greater capacity for challenges to be overcome.

"This," she reports, "is all a result of having reconnected with my second chakra and sexual energy in a new way and really accepting who I have been all along."

Chapter 6
Love

Love is the beauty of the soul.
—Saint Augustine

In our work at TantraNova, we identify love as a state of being in which "I am love," "I love," and "I am loved"; there is no difference between the three. In saying "I am love," we address our capacity not just for expressing love to another person or persons but our ability to experience love as a state of being within, which informs the way we live and love. "I am love" doesn't just mean that we are able and willing to experience love in the sense of romantic love with another person or in the form of familial love for a parent, sibling, and so on. It means we come from a place of compassion and empathy for ourselves and others so we may experience love for ourselves and our fellow travelers. In other words, to use an often-heard phrase, we must love ourselves first so that we may love one another.

"Being love" calls for an evolved state of consciousness. We consider coming to this state central to growing up and maturing as a human being. This requires the willingness and commitment to face ourselves and our survival fears that have us looking for love, attention, and recognition outside ourselves.

How can we access this state of being love? To begin with, we can start listening to the fourth chakra, the love center, the area where the frequency or vibration of the emotion of love originates in our bodies. This center, also known as the heart chakra, is located in the middle of the chest. This should be no surprise—when we feel love, we often experience a warm feeling or openness in the chest. For example, a five-year-old girl exclaims, "Mom, I love you so much," while instinctively placing her hand over her chest bone, her heart center. This is an inner knowingness, given that her heart center is the place where she senses the feeling of love.

The heart or love chakra constitutes the middle of the seven major chakras; three below are oriented toward our earthly existence, and three above are oriented toward our spiritual being. We consider the heart center the reconciler between our physical desires and spiritual penchants. The love center is associated not just with the joy and happiness we experience when in a state of love but also with honesty, respect, compassion, understanding, and generosity.

When the heart center's frequency is off, when there is an energetic block in this chakra, we may say we feel brokenhearted or sad. We may experience pain or discomfort in the chest associated with the loss of a loved one or the ending of a love relationship. When such sensations and energetic blocks are sustained over a prolonged period of time, they can lead to further ailments in our physical, emotional, and spiritual self. This may ultimately turn into a heart attack or lung issues; emotionally we may feel lost, persistently sad, or depressed; mentally we may see ourselves as unlovable and interpret everything that happens around us as being against us. We may view love and those who experience it through a veil of anger or jealousy that can derail us from our journey toward greater wholeness within, and thus from the experience of sexual enlightenment that is an integrated state of our sexual, emotional, and spiritual being.

On the other hand, when the heart center is open and free from blocks, we become more fully connected and integrated within and with others. Life-force energy can flow without restriction from the lower to the upper chakras and back down again. The openness of the heart center is key to integrating our sexual self (the second or creative center) and our spiritual self (the sixth or consciousness center).

Facing and moving beyond our notions and illusions of love such as needing or being dependent on love, we grow into the experience of "being love," or what is also known as "universal love." This is a wisdom that has been around for time immemorial, yet when we are children or adolescents, we often confuse it with the need to complete ourselves or the need for being with another, with romantic love or infatuation. It is important, however, to learn the differences between romantic love, unconditional love, and universal love. Clearing this confusion allows us to live fulfilled and joyous lives.

Romantic Love

Romantic love is the type of love that's been depicted and glorified in fairy tales and Hollywood movies. We fall for another person to whom we feel attracted and with whom we then have an intimate relationship. It is probably regarded as the most common form of love, or at least what we associate with the word *love* as it is used today.

Perhaps the most overarching characteristic of romantic love is that it's conditional—that is, we experience these feelings we know as love for another person as long as that person is pleasing to us and is loving us back. When that person does something we view as wrong or something with which we do not agree—or often for no reason other than we've grown tired of him or her or bored with our relationship—the love we feel can diminish or even disappear altogether. Romantic love is variable in nature, subject to whims and opinions and events. As part of consciously creating love in intimate relationships, romantic love embellishes the connection and joy of being together. In this way it *can* be long-lasting, and it's marvelous when it is.

However, romantic love is not sustainable in itself. There will always be fluctuations; one day we will feel incredibly attracted to our partner physically and emotionally, and the next perhaps we will wish he or she would just leave us alone. In other words, romantic love can be confused with infatuation and often is full of drama, and that is what some people may like most about it. Drama is exciting and enticing; it breaks us out of our boring, everyday lives and allows us to feel something, even though such emotions might not be the most positive or productive. Initially this can seem very appealing, and this is why some may become addicted to a romantic illusion.

Romantic love is externally oriented, receiving its rewards from acknowledgement by another or others. It is ego- or need-based, and we project our own desires and longings onto those with whom we are involved. Jealousy, possessiveness, and control are characteristics of this form of love. Unless we learn practices that allow us to recognize love within us—as defined in *being love*—we will automatically be triggered by another's behaviors and actions into a childlike way of interpreting and experiencing the world of love: I am either loved or not loved by another. Putting space between ourselves and the triggers that control our experience of love is not available to us in the romantic, infatuated state, which is dualistic in nature as in *being loved or not loved*. When our expectations of romantic love are no longer fulfilled, we blame the other for our upsets, our sense of disconnect, or our fear of abandonment. We are doomed to live in unhappy and self-defeating relationships, preventing ourselves from creatively and passionately enjoying our lives.

Romantic, infatuated love can often be related to a collapse of love and sex. In TantraNova terms, we consider this a confusion of the experience between the sexual and love centers: We have sex. It feels so good. We feel being in love. When having sex with another person, there is arousal that leads to a rush of endorphins and hormones, which flood the nervous system with pleasurable sensations and make us feel good—just as we may have felt when being caressed by our mother when being nursed. We felt being loved.

While this phenomenon may appear in men and women, it occurs more frequently for women. Because their physical and emotional wiring is more integrated, women tend to confuse sexual experience with emotional experience more automatically.

In contrast, most males' nervous systems are wired in a way that their bodies and emotions are less integrated because of the difference in the interaction of their right and left brain hemispheres. Men can easily have sex without any heart attachment—to them it can be something they do in order to feel good and make their lives more enjoyable. Some would call this linear way of thinking a form of dissociation, though it clearly is not consciously but biologically and hormonally guided.

Women, on the other hand, are more integrated when it comes to their bodies and emotions and thus are more prone to experience a collapse of the heart and sex centers when involved in a romantic relationship.

For both sexes, the experience of romantic love can be uplifting and exhilarating. In the beginning of a relationship, hormones tend to flow much more actively, bringing about a state of excitement. However, when the hormonal production eases and the excitement wears off after a few months or a couple of years, what are we to do to sustain love and intimacy in a relationship?

Sustaining romantic love in a relationship has to do not only with planning for that romantic dinner or island vacation, which may be lovely and rejuvenating but with evolving into love as a state of being that requires ongoing cultivation through conscious connecting with oneself and one's partner. The practice section in chapter 10 provides such guidance in solo and partner practices.

Unconditional Love

Think about how a mother feels toward her child: she will do anything for him, will defend him, and will always make sure his needs are met. This is not something she does only when he is a baby; this unconditional love a parent has for a child extends throughout both their lives. Essentially, unconditional love is present no matter how the child or teenager behaves or acts. This form of love may appear at times as "tough love," yet always in the context of *being love*. The child is aware of the context even when he may object to the means of delivery.

Unconditional love truly is the glue that holds that relationship together. In fact many parents will note that having a child is what helped them acknowledge the existence of unconditional love in the first place; feeling such unconditional love for another human being opens them up to feeling it for *all* human beings and to recognizing the child—the innocent, wondrous spectator of life—within us all.

Universal Love

Universal love, quite the opposite of romantic love, is never-ending. Also known as "agape," it is unconditional and immune to many of the traps to which romantic love can succumb such as emotions like jealousy or resentment, or one's changing tastes over time. Universal love implies a strong commitment to oneself and a vow to honor, respect, and care for the well-being of another person no matter what situations arise.

When the heart center is completely open and free of blocks, it becomes our means of channeling universal love, which Buddhists refer to as the four kinds of love—loving-kindness, compassion, appreciative joy, and equanimity—and Christians refer to as the Christ consciousness. Universal love is the state of love as a capacity for being present with ourselves and any other human being, transcending sexual, romantic, or infatuated love.

When we open ourselves to universal love, we become more in touch with our divine self, or the spark of divine intelligence that has created all of us, the universe, and life itself. Glimpsing this phenomenon creates a connection, an awareness that enables us to see ourselves in each other, to truly feel the oneness of humankind. This spark allows us to evolve into sustaining love as a practice versus a temporary state of feeling. Being able to experience romantic love, unconditional love, and universal love in an integrated way of being is one of the keys to creating fulfilling lives and relationships.

Falling in Love versus Creating Love

As children, we learn about love and loving from our parents or guardians—the person or people who raise us from the time we are born. As children we experience love when we get the attention we crave, when we feel our caregivers are listening to us and fulfilling our needs. In this way the experience of love is given to us; it is not a conscious process in which we actively participate or that we direct in any way. And this is how we come to believe that love is something that is bestowed upon us by another person or other people, a force outside ourselves that we must seek and gain in order to feel complete.

On the other hand, we may experience the absence of love when our caregiver does not, in our eyes, satisfy our needs. For example, a child may be used to her father coming home from work at the same time each night. Then one night he does not arrive at the usual time. Although he may have been delayed for a number of reasons—a late meeting at work, traffic, a stop at the grocery store, none of which are related to the child—she views his absence as a sign that he does not love her any longer, and she feels abandoned. Such an experience is remembered in the child's nervous system and may determine how she interprets love from that day forward: as a tenuous thing that can disappear at any moment.

These kinds of experiences—we call them *interruptions* in the child's happy and playful world—can become predominant in one's life, carrying over well into adulthood. These nanosecond decisions we make at these moments of interruption become the unconscious drivers for how we experience love or a lack thereof. We play out the same scenarios over and over again: we continue to look for love outside of ourselves. It is the only model we know, and even though it tends to not work very well, we repeat it over and over for lack of a better choice.

Yet there *is* another choice. Instead of constantly falling in love or searching for someone who will fill the emptiness we feel inside ourselves, we want to open ourselves to learning how to create and cultivate love within ourselves. Shifting from "falling in love" to "creating love" may appear foreign and difficult initially. It requires facing the illusion of love being outside oneself and letting go of the attachment to finding love in another. It calls for practices that have us to listen to the heart center, explore, and clear unfulfilled expectations from these early moments in childhood, and return to the self as the origin of one's feelings and emotions.

Connecting with oneself as the source of love alters everything in one's life. This state of being love within allows resonating with another's love. We shift from a pervasive sense of being subjected to, victimized by, or being done to by people, circumstances, or the world at large to a sense of bringing forth our life in love and cocreation.

In the practice section in chapter 10, you will find guidance on how to connect daily with your heart center or develop a regular heart-to-heart connection with your partner. These practices assist us in dropping out of our judgmental, busy mind and into the heart space and feeling love and being loved.

Coming to a State of Love

Over the course of our work with thousands of couples and singles, we have witnessed many of them and heard their intensely personal stories about how they came to create love in their lives.

When Elena came to TantraNova, she shared that she loved falling in love; that feeling of infatuation was a kind of a high for her. She searched it out, usually in men who were not available—they were in relationships, married to other women, or married to their jobs. This meant they were not looking to create lasting relationships with her, and in pursuing them she created an enormous amount of drama in her life. Her affairs were temporary in nature even when they would last for a couple of years and were of excruciating uncertainty.

The romantic feelings were intense, and she enjoyed them at the moment they occurred, but when her lover was not with her she felt lost. She grieved for the attention she was not getting and looked for it over and over again. In fact, she craved it; she did anything to get it. Just like an addict, she never felt satisfied. At that time she didn't have the capacity to untangle herself from this addiction. "Even if I had met a man who was available," she ruminates, "I probably would not have recognized him." She recalls that there was something in the unavailability that had her hooked.

Eventually she fell into a deep depression. Her despair was so grave, she finally acknowledged how far she had sunk, and that something needed to change to pull herself out of this abyss.

For so many years, she had looked for satisfaction through other people, like a Band-Aid she could put on top of a gaping wound. With some self-examination she saw there was something that had a much deeper origin within her, something that was not satisfied or fulfilled. She could not see clearly what it was, but once she knew it was there she was determined to unearth it.

So she put herself on a path to self-discovery by coming to work with us at TantraNova. Through meditation practices she came to face herself and her emotions possibly for the first time. It was startling. The feelings she encountered were excruciating, and she started to see that in fact there was nobody out there who caused these feelings and emotions in her—she was confronted with herself. She learned about the observer state of mind and how to become present to her infatuations, feelings, and behaviors. Letting go of these habitual patterns was a conscious process that ultimately freed her to make better decisions.

What brought her to this state was a very intense clearing process during which she uncovered how she had come to behave as she did. She discovered—and, most importantly, acknowledged—that when she was a child she had been deeply in love with her dad. However, she had always felt as though she was not special to him; she never got enough attention from him. She started to see her deep love for her dad as inextricably connected to her perception of his unavailability. Thus love and unavailability were hooked for her, and that feeling became hardwired in her nervous system.

It continued well into her adulthood until that crucial moment when she began to unhook unavailability from the experience of love. The TantraNova practices of conscious breathing, being in her witness state of mind and reconnecting with her life force energy through sexual healing aided her in releasing the charge around this childhood experience. True freedom arose, and she began to actually love herself. When she didn't need to look for attention anymore to prove to herself she was loved, when she was no longer controlled by the automatic hook, she connected with a deep sense of love within herself, which allowed her to take new and different actions in line with what she wanted to create in her life in terms of love and relationships.

By clearing the confusion around love and unavailability, Elena shifted from her previous state of infatuated romantic love to a state of being love. Within a few months of this opening, she met a man, and their relationship has been unwavering ever since. Love is no longer an experience that traps her but a declaration from which she lives—an inner knowingness that she is love and is loved. It is a state of being she can call on at any time that allows her to know that even if she feels her beloved is not thinking of her, he always loves her.

Elena's story exemplifies the maturation from a childlike experience of love that requires external events to feel loved to the mature state of being love.

Chapter 7
Consciousness

Awareness is the greatest agent for change.
—Eckhart Tolle, *The New Earth*

onsciousness implies a state of awareness of oneself and of the world at large. Conscious awareness allows us human beings to be self-reflective, which includes becoming aware of our own thoughts, feelings, and sensations. As mentioned in chapter 1, we distinguish between the "conscious mind" and the "chatter mind." While the latter can be described as the automatic and undiscerning state of mind, the conscious mind allows us to be focused, intentional, and in control regarding which thoughts or feelings we entertain.

Consciousness on the individual and collective levels has to do with how the world occurs to us and how possibilities are opened or closed to us. It provides the context for what drives our actions and behaviors. The often-cited myth of the flat world as postulated by Copernicus and Columbus in the early 1500s is a great example of witnessing the shift from one context to another—from the view of the world being flat to viewing it as being round. While we can sail around the world in the context of its being considered round, it is impossible to do so in a flat world. The kind of world that is our reference point determines what we see or don't see.

Using this analogy of a flat versus a round world in the context of relationships with oneself and others, we call the phenomenon of not seeing something that always has been there "cognitive blindness." One key purpose of this book is to shed light on the world of sexual-spiritual awareness—or, more specifically, unawareness—and in this way to contribute to removing cognitive blindness. This in turn will allow for greater freedom, joy, and possibility in how we bring forth, experience, and sustain fulfillment in life and relationships.

The conscious or observer mind is discerning and assists in clearing our cognitive blindness, particularly around our sexual, emotional, and interpretive self. The chatter mind, on the other hand, is a state in which our heads are cluttered with worry and doubt, and so full of noise we are unable to hear our own inner wisdom. The chatter mind is scattered and automatic; it darts from here to there, from one topic to the next. Without intervention we are ruled by its automatic assessments of ourselves: we think, *I'm just not good enough*, or *I feel afraid of my overpowering desires*. We may have modeled our feelings and beliefs after our parents', learned them in school, or experienced them on the playground. Through subsequent years of conditioning and familiarity with these thoughts and feelings, we find ourselves in a place of automatic reaction.

As we noted in chapter 3, beliefs and interpretations go hand in hand with sensations such as tightness in the stomach or with emotions such as fear. The chatter mind runs automatically, perpetuating cognitive blindness. For example, as Elena in chapter 6 experienced, when we are accustomed to looking for love outside ourselves, that is what we will return to again and again. It was only through hitting a wall of recurring, deep dissatisfaction in her intimate relationships and waking up to the illusion of love in which she had been living that Elena discovered a new world in terms of love and loving.

With an unrelenting commitment, self-reflection, and willingness to reach beyond the status quo, we can move out of the flat world of instinctive, automatic existence and into a round world where we are at choice to create fulfillment in life, love, and intimacy.

The Consciousness Center

The energy center associated with our conscious being is located in the middle of the forehead, above the eyebrows. It's commonly known as the *third-eye center*. When we are in balance, this center is considered the seat of intuition, intentionality, focus, new ideas, and clarity of thinking. When we are out of balance or energetically blocked, this center can be described as shortsightedness, lack of vision, being in one's head, or being run by one's desires and emotions.

Through the consciousness center, we can see ourselves as both creations and creators, as being of universal consciousness and as conscious, sentient beings, as connected to all things and beings around us in the world at large and as solitary beings. It is this sense of belonging and, at the same time, autonomy that defines us as conscious human beings; it does not just influence our experiences and views of our internal and external environments, but creates them.

Perception is subject to our state of consciousness, which is formed and molded by ancestral confluence, societal beliefs, early childhood experiences, and what we have learned since then. In the context of this book, we are particularly interested in the perception and consciousness of ourselves as sexual and love beings. Frequently the experiences of sex and love are considered things that *happen to us* versus *us creating the experiences.* By bringing consciousness to life-force sexual energy (the second chakra or creation center) and to love (the fourth chakra or heart center), we step off the flat world of being subjected to some way of feeling or being and into the round world of sensing, witnessing, and shaping our feelings and ways of being. Hence we can say that consciousness is really fused with the heart and creation centers.

When we integrate these three energy centers or dimensions of our being—sex, love, and consciousness—we create lasting fulfillment and intimacy in life. They are interdependent, one no more important than another. Through the focused mind we can channel sexual energy from the creation center to the heart center, integrating our experiences and expressions of sexual pleasure and love. We can move sexual energy as well from the creation to the consciousness center, fueling our intentions and imbuing our visions with creative life-force energy.

In this way we bring consciousness to accessing our sexual energy in a state that goes far beyond procreation, which is the biological purpose of sexual life-force energy that perpetuates the existence of the human species. By using our life-force energy beyond reproduction, we evolve to create and cocreate our lives and relationships.

When we are in an aroused sexual state, the chemicals in our body are in flux, causing us to become more loving, more vulnerable, and more open not only to expressions of love and sex in various forms but to oneself, one's partner, and the essence of life itself. In this process of becoming more conscious of our sexual energy through specifically designed practices, we get to see and clear any constrictions, blocks, or interpretations such as shame, fear, or guilt.

When we consciously open ourselves in this way and see what was previously obscured or hidden—as in our own sexual energy and how we can use it to create more joy and passion in our lives—we open ourselves to something that can be incredibly powerful: choice. When we are in this state of allowing sexual energy to flow through us, being aware of the effects it can have on us, and using it to create more joy and creativity in our lives, we can say we are at will: we are making decisions that affect our lives and choosing whether to stay mired in our old habits and misunderstandings or to move forward into conscious awareness that can bring us that much closer to the state of sexual enlightenment.

Taking off the Shades

Jay came to TantraNova at a time in his life when he was looking to make shifts in his career and personal relationships. After fifteen years of being in the insurance business, where he had greatly accelerated, he no longer felt fulfilled and missed a sense of purpose in his life. He felt stagnant, bored, and disconnected from himself and his creativity. He felt deeply dissatisfied.

Jay knew it was time to change. "I was soul dead and kept asking myself, *What do I do well?*" For a long time, he had been dreaming of becoming an actor; however, he had never taken serious steps toward it. In his personal relationships, he had been chasing the illusion of intimacy while staying aloof with and detached from women and trying to be in control at all times.

Yes, controlling his environment and manipulating the outcomes he desired were his modus operandi. This kept him in a kind of isolated and armored state physically and emotionally. The first big step for Jay was to start to face himself and see the protective shield he had appropriated. One of the things that came to light in his work at TantraNova was what he called the "ego wars" he would experience within himself. He described feelings of aggression and anger at times when dealing with other men or when he felt challenged by another. He began to acknowledge that he always felt as if he had to be on guard and ready for attack. Through particular exercises and processes he engaged in during our workshops, he got to experience himself and see his own behaviors in the dynamic with others, such as the social and interpersonal games he played or the way he seduced others just for the sake of self-gratification without any commitment to engaging more deeply.

Once Jay became more aware of his armoring and self-protection, which he had disguised with a cool, macho kind of appearance, he was willing to open himself to the feelings and emotions that were hidden underneath that shell. His focus shifted from how he could manipulate the world in order to get what he thought he wanted to becoming courageous enough to acknowledge his uncomfortable feelings and the sense of vulnerability he had avoided for most of his life. By opening himself to himself, he connected to his heart chakra (the fourth center) and tapped into a listening to himself that had not been accessible to him until then.

In this process of self-realization and opening to his feelings and vulnerable self, Jay started to examine his relationship with his sexual being and how he had used his prowess to impress, coerce, and pull women into his sphere. While going through the foundational coursework at TantraNova, he became more conscious of his life-force energy and started to exercise and master his ejaculatory reflex (see the sexual healing practices in chapter 10). This in turn enabled him to channel his orgasmic energy up into his heart and third-eye centers.

"By doing the pelvic-floor muscle squeeze," he says, "I ignite my sexual energy and can feel it stir my lower chakras. It's the sensation that awakens arousal and desire. Through practice, focus, and guided breath, I am now able to channel the arousal throughout my whole being. This allows me to sustain and connect more deeply with myself solo or with my beloved in partner sex. It also allows me to transmute that vital and pleasant energy into my acting career and goals."

The simple and delightful experience Jay describes is evidence of the power that lies integrated within the body, mind, and spirit of every one of us. It is the manifestation of channeled creative energy, vibrant sexuality, and connection to the oneness that we are.

"This is the gateway to being able to get the more-subtle impact of the TantraNova practices that bring consciousness to my sexual being," Jay explains. "It all starts here."

Learning to ground himself in his sexual center versus being driven by that center made a huge difference in how he started to experience himself. Jay uses the pelvic-floor muscle practice (see chapter 10) to build strength and enhance performance by retaining ejaculate, but also to remain grounded in emotionally triggering situations.

He describes that at first, working with his pelvic-floor muscles was challenging and that he would get tired easily. "It's just like any other muscle—it takes time to build and strengthen. It pulls you into yourself and forces you to look at what's there, and to sit with the inner core of your being. At first it may be uncomfortable."

Jay describes his transformation as "taking my sunglasses off on a bright day. At first I was uncomfortable and wanted to shield my eyes, but as I adjusted and left the tinted view behind, I could see with more clarity. I'm *alive*!"

Raising Consciousness

In part, the dictionary definition of consciousness is "awareness: especially concern for some social or political cause." This too applies to our work at TantraNova as our goal is to raise awareness of our social fabric with respect to how we both relate to and misunderstand sexual energy. We envision that as more people become conscious of sexual energy and the ways in which they can tap into it and utilize it to create joyous and fulfilling lives and relationships, the mores and beliefs of our culture and our society will shift toward embracing a more loving, open, and productive atmosphere that is inclusive of and beneficial to all humankind.

First, however, we must start with ourselves and with those who are closest to us. When we at TantraNova assist people in becoming conscious of sexual energy, we call it a *rediscovery* because this energy has always been there; we come to see how integral it is to our lives whether we are aware of it or not. This life force has been running through us all along; we simply bring people's attention to it and teach them how to engage with it in ways that will empower them to create what they want in their lives. In teaching this consciousness, we move sexual energy from something that goes on automatically within and all around us to a force with which we can actively engage in order to fuel our thoughts, sensations, and feelings in ways we never have before. Indeed, many people have not even been aware that this possibility exists.

Without the capacity to be conscious, we would not—could not—become aware of life-force sexual energy in our lives. Consciousness may be seen as an access that allows us to pry open the lid and let the sexual energy out so we may work with it to build more joy, passion, and creativity in everything we do.

This involves learned practices of the sort we teach in our workshops, some of which we will detail in chapter 10. Through these practices we invoke and channel sexual energy in order to boost our physical health and well-being, enhance our emotional balance and love connections, and turbo-charge our dreams and visions. In this meditative state of sexual, heart, and spirit connection within and with a beloved, peace, joy, and bliss are available, giving rise to sexual enlightenment.

Chapter 8
Conscious Evolution

⁓᠂⤜⟢᠂⁓

The human species can, if it wishes, transcend itself.
—Julian Huxley, *New Bottles for New Wine*

Sexual enlightenment is a key aspect of evolving ourselves as humanity. While some evolutionary theory and systems emphasize the need for *spiritual* evolution at this time and in this age, we consider becoming *sexually* evolved just as crucial and an integral dimension of evolving ourselves and our coexistence on this planet. Andrew Cohen, the founder of Evolutionary Enlightenment and coauthor of the article "Is Sex a Path to God?" calls sexual life-force energy "the physical expression of the *evolutionary impulse* behind this entire universe. What could be more powerful than that?"

Yet sexual life-force energy is the least understood and most convoluted form of energy. In our view, the imperative of conscious evolution calls for and embraces the integration of the sexual, emotional, and spiritual self.

Barbara Marx Hubbard's quote from *Birth 2012 and Beyond* in chapter 1—"Evolution is evolving from unconscious chance to conscious choice"—reminds us that we have choice in affecting our continued existence on this planet. *The "evolutionary impulse" includes bringing consciousness to our sexual life-force energy. We shift from being unconsciously at the effect of this energy to consciously choosing to evolve ourselves through this energy.* Without becoming aware of the evolutionary impulse as a source to consciously create and cocreate from, we would continue perpetuating the sole view of "biological evolution" as identified by Charles Darwin. Darwin's discoveries in human and animal development form the basis of what is now considered our biological heritage. That sort of evolution—the concept of our bodies and their capabilities adapting to our surroundings over time in order to help us survive in an ever-changing environment—is well accepted and proven. We are part of this universal consciousness and cosmic intelligence.

What do we mean by "unconscious chance"? The state of this condition can be likened to a fish in the water: it lives in the water as a function of its being, as it requires the water for its respiration and other bodily processes. In that sense the fish is one with the water. Without it the fish's survival would be endangered. Our relationship to our sexual life-force energy can be described as a state of unconscious chance, a symbiosis similar to what the fish has with water. However, unlike the fish, the evolved human capacity to self-reflect allows us to notice and become aware of "water" and thus transcend our relationship by creating with our sexual life-force energy rather than merely being subjected to it.

It reminds us of Victor Frankle, the Austrian psychiatrist who survived the Holocaust, saying, "Between stimulus and response there is a space. In that space is our power to choose our response. In our response lies our growth and our freedom."

The Need for an Evolutionary Shift

Sexual consciousness is not the only component of bringing about a shift in human evolution, but it is one of the main keys to opening the door. Unless we bring consciousness to sexual life-force energy, the evolutionary impulse, the Force, the spark of life—whatever we want to call it—we may devolve instead of evolve. This is a strong claim to make, so let's explain why we say this.

Frequently, when an evolutionary shift is about to happen, historic unconsciousness reveals itself by the occurrence of breakdowns. We consider breakdowns occurring in the status quo part of the evolutionary shift just as hairline fractures in a building's foundation will, over a very long time, eventually lead to a structural collapse. In the same way, we look at the public attention recently given to political sex scandals, sexual abuse, sexual harassment, the sex trade, high divorce rates, and so on as an indicator that something is shifting in the collective consciousness. We are waking up and facing what will no longer be tolerated. This is the forbearer of the quantum leap from sexual unconsciousness to sexual consciousness.

Here are a few examples of breakdowns that have been revealed over the past twenty years that may be indicators of an impending shift as we see it:

Extramarital affairs in politics were kept discrete in the 1960s, though we know now of JFK's alleged adultery; in the 1990s President Clinton was impeached for lying about the same behavior.

For centuries sexual abuse of minors by priests has been present in the Catholic Church—yet not until recently have abuse victims come forward to bring light to this horrific condition.

Sexual harassment has been pervasive in the workplace— however, it was not brought forward until the early 1990s via the confirmation hearings of Clarence Thomas for Supreme Court justice.

Prostitution has been around forever; however, attention to the sex trade in the United States and around the world did not increase until a few years ago.

For millennia the dominant structure of gender relationships has been based on a hierarchical model. It wasn't until the advent of the women's movement that we began to question gender inequality in the intimate, familial, work, and political spheres.

As a society we are in unknown territory as far as creating fulfilling and sustainable relationships are concerned and find ourselves with a staggering number of broken marriages and a high rate of divorce.

How did we get here? Sexual awareness has been enshrouded in perpetual unconsciousness over the millennia. For example, the epidemic of sexual abuse is a product of denying that sexual energy exists or pretending that it doesn't. This denial or pretense leaves a vacuum in guiding and educating the young and the old in creating a conscious relationship with their life-force energy. In our current system, the locker room, online porn, or a first experience of having sex provides the classroom for learning (in an awkward way) about our life force, or the Divine spark. For generations we have been missing skills for harnessing our energy and consciously expressing it, and this has left most of us feeling fear, guilt, or shame about this most powerful source.

For example, take the Catholic Church, which requires priests to practice celibacy. On one hand this practice can be most beneficial when it is chosen; on the other hand, without learning to transmute this pleasurable, powerful life-force energy in a conscious way through learned practices, suppression or repression of that energy can turn into aberrant behaviors looking for outlets in inappropriate ways.

Another example of this unconsciousness is sexual addiction, which usually has to do with avoiding uncomfortable feelings we don't want to feel. Just as with any other addictive behavior, acting on sexual addiction gives temporary relief. Over time the addicted person becomes self-absorbed and less and less able to truly connect with himself or herself or relate intimately and sexually with another. For instance, with easy access to porn, men who masturbate incessantly, as we have found in our professional practice, require rougher and rougher stimulation in order to get aroused—to feel something—which in turn desensitizes their nerve endings and deadens the capacity for physical and emotional relating. As a consequence, these men grow incapable of authentically connecting and being intimately present with themselves and their partners.

There are areas in our society where harnessing sexual life-force energy is applied as a practice, as in sports or the military. Athletic coaches encourage their male players to refrain from ejaculating for one to several days before a game so they will not expend their precious energy and thus are more available to focus acutely and enhance endurance during competition.

In the US military during wartime, soldiers are isolated and deprived of expressing their sexual selves through restrictions on physical sexual contact. This repressed sexual energy fuels drive and determination and may be channeled into aggression. It all comes down to the intention with which we use our sexual life-force energy—to destruct or construct humanity.

Our point is that energy can be channeled in different ways based on choice. While utilizing sexual drive to affect certain outcomes in sports and the military, sexual consciousness is not being cultivated in the confines of either field as evidenced by recurring incidences of rape and sexual harassment.

Male and Female Sexual Energy

Throughout history men have owned women via their sexual behavior. A man's role used to be the hunter who brought home the food for the family, the builder who constructed shelter to keep them safe, and the security guard who kept any and all threats away from his women and children. Primitive man's main focus was to procreate and propagate the human species—an act he carried out unconsciously as a biological imperative. In order to be attractive to a man and thus gain his protection in what could often be a dangerous environment, women—also unconsciously—would use their sexual energy to attract and keep partners.

This dynamic has become socialized over time, and though we no longer rely on hunting and building for our domestic needs, we continue with these gender stereotypes. Modern men are heralded for their sexual prowess and conquests from an early age; when a teenage boy experiences sex for the first time, he may tell his father, who will reaffirm the boy's virility by congratulating him and giving him condoms—a tacit approval of what he's done and an implication that the boy is on his path to manhood.

On the other hand, when a teenage girl has sex for the first time, often she will keep it secret out of shame or embarrassment. She most likely will not go to her mother for fear of disapproval and being considered impure or no longer marriage material. In some parts of the world, she may be called a whore, outcast from her family or community, or even stoned to death.

This historical disparity in celebrating male sexual energy and vilifying female sexual energy is another symptom of our lack of understanding of sexual life-force energy. If greater consciousness is brought to sustaining masculine energy and reawakening feminine energy, deeper listening and presence can occur for the male, and expanded joy and aliveness can be experienced by the woman. In chapter 10 we will expand on how to learn and cultivate this way of being as part of the "Sexual Healing Practices for the Woman and the Man" practice series.

The Divine Spark

Sexual energy creates life. Through it we have evolved from single-celled amoebae into multicellular organisms, and into bipedal Homo sapiens who are capable of conscious thought. And now, by evolving from unconscious chance to conscious choice, we have the opportunity to participate consciously in and affect the evolutionary process by allowing ourselves to be aware of this divine spark and choosing to use it to our personal advantage and growth, as well as for the greater good of our fellow travelers and, indeed, our planet.

For many people this is a completely foreign concept as they continue to view sexual energy as having to do only with the actual sex act. However, if we bring consciousness to this energy, intercourse and other forms of physical sex can become conscious and blissful expressions of that energy. Furthermore, intercourse may not even be necessary when we learn to transcend the energy to integrate our sexual, emotional, mental, and spiritual being— to experience what we have coined "sexual enlightenment" (see chapter 1).

Sexual or life-force energy is at the core of actualizing Divine intelligence within ourselves and humankind at large. It is up to us to choose to make the quantum leap from unconscious carnality to a world where we can live fulfilled lives in greater harmony and cocreation. As humans we have broken barriers in the industrial, technological, and medical fields. We can live in space and send robots to Mars; we can move hundreds of thousands of people and millions of tons of equipment across continents and oceans to fight wars. However, to feed the hungry on our planet, to get clean water to people in developing countries, to live in peace amongst nations, races, and religions, to stop the cruelty perpetrated against women and children, we are called to make this sexual-spiritual leap so we can see ourselves in each other.

The evolution that needs to take place lies in our willingness—and, more importantly, our choice—to allow sexual consciousness to transform unconscious sexual lust and suppression, and our correlated emotions and interpretations. *Sexual enlightenment is not about intercourse making the world a better place. It's about what sexual energy means to us as a creative force of existence and how by listening to it we can bring consciousness to our sexual energetic selves and create greater physical, emotional and spiritual health and well-being.* This in turn opens the door to feeling more joyful, creative, passionate, peaceful, and hopeful in our relationships and in the world.

Release
the Day
Therapeutic Massage

Rosa Casas,
NCTMB
96 Roosevelt Street
St. Charles IL 60174
630-234-5855

PART III

A Call to Action

Chapter 9
Beyond Talking

❧❧❧

The intimacy that arises in listening ... is only possible
if we can open to the vulnerability of our own hearts.
—Tara Brach, *True Refuge*

Clearing Residual Memory

How can we tap into experiences from a time when we had no language to name them, from when we were infants and perhaps even from before we were born? What life-altering experiences may we have had in adolescence that we felt deeply and coped with through denial? In those periods we may not have been able to communicate or express ourselves, but that does not mean we could not feel.

To bring these memories to the surface, we at TantraNova have developed particular somatic and energy-based practices to access subconscious memory through sensory experiences. These practices serve in the process of clearing what may hold us back from creating what we want in our lives and relationships.

The brain is divided into two hemispheres. The left hemisphere is responsible for logical and analytical thinking as well as linguistic capacities. The right hemisphere is related to creativity, emotions, artistic expression, and feelings. The TantraNova practices allow us to go beyond left-brain, linear thinking to the right-brain hemisphere in order to access residual memory stored at the cellular level—including the sexual center— that cannot be accessed through the conscious analytical mind.

This is how Elena began to explore what kept her from having a fulfilling and joyful relationship (see chapter 6 for more of her story). Initially she approached the issue through talk therapy, which assisted her in feeling heard and encouraged to speak, exploring her feelings, and letting go of them. However, the condition underlying her struggles in relationships— unconsciously carried over from childhood experiences with her dad not being available—was unidentifiable to her on a conscious level and hidden on the cellular level of her sexual-emotional self.

While the modality of talk therapy was useful in opening the door to herself, Elena had not shifted the underlying cellular memory of a deep sense of feeling all alone, separate, and vulnerable. In order to protect herself and avoid ever feeling so vulnerable again, she continued the unconscious pattern of being attracted to unavailable men. This attraction was a reflection of her emotional unavailability and distrust, which were invisible to her.

It was only through in-depth sexual-emotional healing work that Elena tapped in to that wounded place of feeling so alone, helpless, and forgotten. The "Sexual Healing Practice for the Woman" (see practice six in chapter 10) allowed her to access and reexperience the uncomfortable feelings of abandonment of her early childhood experience with her dad. Repressed physical and emotional energy that lay dormant was released. What was opened up for Elena through this healing experience was a clearing of an old imprint in the subconscious that no longer served her. She came to a new sense of clarity and trust within herself and subsequently experienced a deeper trust in men in general.

This fundamental shift altered the way Elena started to view the original childhood experience and the story she had held of herself as a girl and woman. We call this a *shift in cellular and emotional frequency,* where the static of the wounded self gets cleared and a recalibration occurs that allows for a sense of wholeness and unity within. This opened up a new possibility: Six months later Elena met her beloved partner.

Shifting Interpretation

Living a sexually enlightened life is a process of moving beyond what we've habitually done and listening more deeply to our inner voice—an inner knowingness—that can be heard only when we become still enough to get in touch and reconnect with our creative selves and our passion.

By now it has become clear that the TantraNova approach is designed to assist people—singles and couples—in connecting with their authentic selves and tapping into their full self-expression to realize their potential and to live fulfilled lives. This calls for a major transformational shift that involves, on the one hand, a willingness to clear the subconscious places that lie dormant within us yet determine the results we get in our lives, and on the other hand an increased awareness of the chatter mind and all it entails in regard to coming to stillness. The latter includes cultivating one's witness or observer state of mind; becoming less affected by feelings, emotions, or fleeting desires; and shifting debilitating interpretations of oneself and one's past experiences. In a nutshell it means stepping out of feeling subjected to life and stepping into authoring one's life.

Through the clearing of physical-sexual, emotional, and spiritual constrictions and the recalibration of the axis of sex, love, and consciousness as indicated in the ancient traditions of Tantra and Taoism, we can return to a sense of unity and wholeness within.

Furthermore, we draw on Western forms of philosophy such as hermeneutics, through which we can become aware of our automatic listening and interpretations of sex, romance, infatuation, intimacy, love, and commitment. What we say and how we express ourselves verbally and nonverbally reveals the context that determines our behaviors and outlook on life. This lays the foundation for examining the status quo of how consciously and by choice—or not—we bring about the relationship with ourselves and others. In turn, this opens the door to seeing new possibilities and creating new choices for how to view and live one's life.

Think about how many aspects of your sexuality are simply interpretations of what you have gleaned either implicitly or subconsciously from your family, friends, society, and so on and have continued believing unquestioned because "that's just how it is." Consider the notion of love that is instilled culturally through ancient fairy tales, such as Snow White being awakened by the prince, or modern-day movies, such as *Pretty Woman* being saved by the wealthy businessman from a working-girl life.

Sexuality, and thus sexual energy, is perhaps the arena in which we hold the most and largest unconscious, unquestioned interpretations simply because it has been enshrouded in shame, fear, and guilt for millennia. You might not even realize there is an alternative to the way in which you interface with sexual energy and utilize it—or not—to create a fulfilling life for yourself.

Generative versus Reactive

In our TantraNova workshops, we regularly ask the participants how they feel after completing a practice. Frequently the answer is something like, "Looking into my partner's eyes made me feel awkward," or "It felt really good." Either answer assigns one's feelings to an external source—in this case the partner or an "it"—and misses that feelings, sensations, and emotions originate from within the speaker. We live in a helpless state when we assume we are at the mercy of other people or events, and as such our nervous systems get wired from childhood to believe that this is how we are to experience and interpret our world. Thus the helplessness is perpetuated and becomes a way of living in which we never truly own the emotions we feel or even take credit for producing them. In becoming the author of our experiences, we shift to declaring how "I feel," as in "I felt awkward" or "I feel good."

When we have spent our whole lives believing others cause our emotions—*he* made me angry, or *she* makes me happy—it can be difficult initially to see the world and our inner selves any other way. However, *letting go of notions that no longer serve us is a key aspect of coming to see ourselves as the authors of our own lives in order to create fulfilling and conscious relationships.* Here we can see that language is generative in nature and not merely descriptive, as we alluded to in chapter 3 regarding speech act theory.

Creativity and Pleasure

Let's recall the premise we laid out in chapter 1: *When life force or sexual energy is unencumbered and free of past personal stories and collective interpretations that no longer serve us, creativity and pleasure are more accessible to us everywhere in life.* A primary access to creativity and pleasure is learning sexual consciousness practices as we have described them throughout this book. To enhance the process, we make use of a methodology called creative self-discovery involving music, movement, and drama (see *Creative Self Discovery: A Journey into Self-Consciousness* by Fred Weaver III, MD). The role the arts play in pursuing one's sexual enlightenment cannot be overestimated, for it is when we are creating, in whatever way comes naturally to us, that we can begin to let go of what seems so predictable and move into an improvisational sort of dream state of infinite possibility.

Ultimately, creative self-discovery is as much about discovering what we love to do for ourselves as it is about revealing what unique contributions we can make to the world. Perhaps you love gardening and simply focus on your garden, as it is the one passion through which you feel happy expressing yourself, and deep down you do want to experience joy. So you tend to your flowers and shrubs with love. You pour all your time and effort into your garden, and you create a sight that is truly breathtaking to behold, full of life and vibrant color, a scene that would make anyone stop to take a look.

And you find this is just what's happening: your garden has

become so large and so beautiful that people walking by on the sidewalk pause to comment on it and just stand and take it in, always leaving with smiles on their faces. By following your passion, you have inspired others.

Chapter 10
The Practices

You do not need to know everything to get going.
Just get into the game. You will learn by doing.
—Jack Canfield, *The Success Principles*

How does one cultivate sexual enlightenment? We have given you lots of insights and information into what sexual enlightenment is and what difference it can make in people's lives and relationships. The foundational practices now laid out in this chapter and available via the corresponding audio download will assist you in laying the foundation for your own journey into sexual enlightenment.

The practices build on each other, so we recommend you follow them in sequence. This will support you in making them your own and assure that you get the most from your practice.

| *Practice 5* | Yin and Yang: Balancing Feminine and Masculine Energy Practice |
| *Practice 6* | Sexual Healing Practices for the Woman and the Man |

Practices 1 through 5 are available via free audio download at http://www.tantranova.com/foundational-practices.html.

Practice 6 is available as a home-study audio and video program at www.tantranova.com/intimacy-products/intimacy-dvds.html.

Practice 1: Calm the Unending Chatter in Your Mind
Conscious Breathing Practice

Benefits:
Coming to stillness and inner peace
Feeling connected with yourself
Developing the capacity to be in the present moment
Cultivating the observer state of mind

Remember what we said about conscious breath in chapter 1: *Using breath consciously as a tool is the first step to entering the mindful world of sexual energy. When we are present with our breath, we can reach a place of focus, stillness, and inner peace that allows us to go deeper into ourselves and our experiences.*

For example, when feeling angry, a common response is to "see red" or "lose your head" and become so angry it takes over every part of your consciousness. By using conscious breathing in moments like these, you can retain your sense of self and your clarity of mind and be aware that you feel angry, giving space and distance to the state of feeling instead of being swept away by the feeling. This is the difference between *"I am angry!"* and *"I feel anger."* In the former, the anger is so much a part of your state of being that it becomes who you are just as you might say, "Hi, I'm George." Mindfully, through focus and breath, you can separate yourself and become the observer of your feelings so that *"I'm angry"* is changed to "I am George and I feel angry." Breath is the key to unlocking the inner worlds of yourself in order to live from a place of peace. It is only from this place of calm and peace that we can sit with ourselves, know ourselves, and then begin to know another.

Marianne is a fresh-faced, twenty-five-year-old woman just getting her feet wet in her first counseling job. She is independent, responsible, and motivated. Since high school she has always had a boyfriend and referred to herself as a "serial monogamist." She related that having a boyfriend gave her the chance to express her loving, nurturing, caring side, which was very much part of her joy. When one relationship fell apart for some reason or another, Marianne was often quick to find someone else to fill that need for feeling love and being loved.

She had left her past relationship feeling disappointed, annoyed, confused, and jaded about love. She described how she always put so much into a relationship and the other person but never got enough back from her partner. She would take the initiative to set up dates and romantic outings and always gave the best and most-thoughtful gifts. She thought of herself as good at relationships and a great partner and probably was for many of the men she dated, yet Marianne always felt unfulfilled by her partners. She often noticed their faults and very rarely recognized her own feelings, expectations, and behaviors that contributed to the lost spark and ending of a relationship. Not one of her partners was able to give her what she gave them or satisfy her need for feeling loved.

Upon moving to Chicago during one of her rare stretches as a single, Marianne was introduced to TantraNova and started working with conscious breath, energy awareness, and the "observer." She learned to be present in the moment and develop that nonjudgmental observer of her thoughts, feelings, and behaviors. Marianne saw that although her partners weren't perfect, they weren't all to blame either. She started sharing that she might be looking to others to love and be loved because there was something within herself that felt empty and craved love and attention. In one realization she made the connection that perhaps it wasn't that her partners didn't love her enough but that she didn't love, nurture, and care for herself enough. She noticed that she had often lost herself in her love relationships and had been so busy showering her partners with love as an avoidance of feeling emptiness, loneliness, and discomfort within herself.

We use breath as a guide to come to the present moment in the TantraNova approach. This allows us to become like the moose in chapter 1 walking through the forest, and it allows the inner *observer, watcher,* or *witness* of one's feeling states, emotions, physical sensations, and conversations to arise. Without focus and intention, the mind goes on automatic chatter, making up stories and meanings incessantly. In his book *A New Earth: Awakening to Your Life's Purpose,* Eckhart Tolle says, "The primary cause of unhappiness is never the situation but your thoughts about it. Be aware of the thoughts you are thinking. Separate them from the situation, which is always neutral, which always is as it is."

In the "moose," or witness state, one gets to be connected with oneself and to tap into stillness and peace—and that's the space where we find intimacy. We invite you to connect with your "moose" by offering the following practice:

The Practice

Sit comfortably in a chair or on a cushion on the floor.

Close your eyes.

Place your right hand on your belly right below the navel.

Exhale all air, emptying yourself out.

Now take a deep breath into the nose, down the trachea, and all the way down into your belly, expanding your belly like a big balloon.

Exhale back up and out at your own pace, depth, and rhythm.

Again take a deep breath into the belly, extending your belly like a big balloon into your hand.

On the exhalation visualize sending the breath back up and out. Notice your belly flattening.

Continue breathing in this pattern for a total of ten breaths. Witness the rising of your belly on the inhalation and the falling of your belly on the exhalation.

Upon completion notice how you feel and how your body feels. Become aware of any sensations and your state of mind at the present moment.

Practice 2: Circulating Energy
Chakra Listening Practice

Benefits:
Deepening the listening to your energy centers
Tuning in to your feelings and state of being
associated with each energy center
Moving energetic breath

Shhh ... do you hear that? No, not the sound of the traffic outside the window, and no, not the kids playing in the other room. Try again, but this time use the ears of your inner listener. Become quiet for a moment and turn your attention inward. Do you hear *you*?

   This practice is designed to help you gain a better awareness and understanding of your energy centers or dimensions of being and feeling, and the power of circulating energy through each center. It will work to open and focus your mind to each part of your energetic being and shed light on the blockages and/or power that may reside in each chakra.

As you go through this practice, be open to listening to yourself: How do you feel? Where does the feeling reside in your body? What emotion or experience is the feeling tied to? There may be times when you've heard that little voice in your head or your intuition pointing the way, and you may or may not have listened. Now is your opportunity to check in and see what your body and your being are telling you.

Listen. Just as in any communication practice, there is a difference between hearing and listening. We *hear* noises, words, inflection, and accents. When we *listen* we go beyond the sound and consciously concentrate on the meaning of what we hear. In communicating with others and ourselves, we are not often hard of hearing but rather hard of listening.

Each chakra is connected to dimensions of our being and experiencing. When we are on- or off-target in areas associated with a chakra, the energy in the center will change—for example when we are rendered speechless by a feeling of shock or disempowerment, or when we are in love and feel the swell of emotion near our heart. Focusing on each center opens up the chakras and allows energy to move through them via breath.

In the later part of the exercise, we start to move energy in circulation through the chakras, therefore uniting them into a state of aliveness! Using breath to move energy is the essential magic of this practice, and it starts with circulating your own energy through you. When we circulate energy, we feel a sense of wholeness, peace and being at home in our body and being.

Each center has something to say—a story to tell and a song to sing. By becoming intent on listening, we hear past the buzz, past the distracting thoughts, past the numbness, or past the pain and connect with the melody of our true selves. The melody may be melancholy blues, romantic R&B, or spunky rock and roll, but it is what provides us information about where our strengths and tender areas are in the moment of awareness. Each chakra becomes an instrument in an orchestra, and with the breath as the conductor, the music of transcendence is performed.

Billy started doing the Chakra Listening Practice daily as part of his ongoing work at TantraNova after experiencing an opening and illumination in areas of his mind, body, and spirit, which had grown dark over the years. In the beginning of Billy's journey into Tantra, he discovered the importance of opening up and becoming integrated with himself and his energy since he had grown up in a very conservative, sexually repressed environment.

Billy describes that when he was first building awareness through the Chakra Listening Practice, he discovered that while his upper chakras (the heart, throat, and third-eye) were quite strong, he noticed blockages in his lower root, creation, and solar plexus centers. Throughout the practice, as Billy began to listen and get to know his different energies and awaken his sexual energetic flow, he experienced feelings of guilt. Through his listening and willingness to work to understand and dig through his feelings, he discovered repressed memories of sexual abuse by a religious leader in his past. His body and spirit had remembered and clung on to what his mind had forgotten.

The Chakra Listening Practice helped open the door for healing and awareness so Billy could clear the emotional and energetic blockages that were keeping him from creating the life he desired. Billy described how, through continuous support from and further work with TantraNova, he was able to "travel through the darkness and the fear and come out on the other side." Billy continues to do the Chakra Listening Practice daily as a check-in and to gain "greater relaxation, peace, and fluidity" in his entire being. The practice provides grounding, balancing, and crucial information on the state of our body, mind, and spirit as well as the blockages that keep body, mind, and spirit from functioning as an integrated whole.

Billy states that he now feels more flow and openness for his sexual, creative energy and therefore more freedom to create the relationships and life he desires. He advises those starting out with this practice to face the blockages, barriers, or baggage that may come in the melody your chakras sing and to "have faith that things will turn out well in the end," just as he had experienced.

The Practice

Sit comfortably in a chair or on a cushion on the floor

Base center

Place your right hand under your buttocks from the front, sitting on your fingers.

Take in a deep breath, expanding the belly like a big balloon.

On exhalation send the breath down and out the buttocks into the hand.

Again take in a deep breath, breathing into the belly, expanding the belly like a big balloon.

On exhalation visualize sending the breath down and out of the butt into the hand.

Continue this breathing pattern.

The air comes in through the nose, goes down the windpipe into the lungs, and returns up and out on the exhalation. So when we say "sending the breath down and out," we use our inner focus and eye to visualize sending the energetic breath down and out of the butt into the hand.

The area where your hand rests is called the "root chakra," or "base center." It is connected with groundedness, centeredness, and a sense of security within. When we are constrained energetically in the base center, we may experience fear of survival; being afraid of not being good enough or not having enough; or worrying about the future. By breathing into your base center, you allow yourself to connect with your inner groundedness and centeredness and a sense of security within.

Creation Center

Place your right hand above the pubic bone, below the navel.

When you are ready, exhale all air.

Take in a deep breath, filling the belly and extending the belly into the hand.

On exhalation send the breath down and out of the base center, into the cushion of the chair.

Again breathe in, opening the belly into the hands.

On exhalation send the breath down and out of the base center, into the cushion of the chair.

Continue this breathing pattern.

The area where your hand rests is called the "second chakra," or "creation center." It is connected with your creative self, pleasure, joy for life, and aliveness. When you are constrained energetically in the creation center, you may experience a disconnect from your creative or pleasure self, or diminished joy or aliveness. By breathing into your creation center, you allow yourself to connect with your creative, pleasurable, joyous, and alive self.

Power Center

Place your right hand in the middle of your upper belly, on the solar plexus below the ribcage.

Exhale all air when you are ready. Take in a deep breath, filling the belly. Now the upper belly extends into the hand. On exhalation send the breath down and out of the base center into the cushion of the chair.

Again breathe in, opening the upper belly into the hand. On exhalation send the breath down and out of the first center into the cushion of the chair.

Continue this breathing pattern.

The area where your hand rests is called the "third chakra," or "power center." It is connected with inner personal power, willpower, and fortitude. When we are constrained energetically in the power center, we may experience a sense of helplessness or powerlessness, anger or frustration, or a need for control. By breathing into your power center, you allow yourself to connect with your inner personal power, willpower, and fortitude.

Heart Center

If you care to switch your hands, place your left hand now in the middle of your chest, between your breasts.

When you are ready, exhale all air. Take in a deep breath, filling the belly then all the way up into the chest, opening the chest into the hands.

On exhalation send the breath down through your torso and out of the base center into the cushion of the chair.

Again breathe in, opening the chest into the hand.

On exhalation send the breath down and out of the first center into the cushion of the chair.

Continue this breathing pattern.

The area where your hand rests is called the "fourth chakra," or "heart center." It is connected with love and compassion for yourself first and foremost and then for another. When we are constrained energetically in the heart center, we may experience prolonged sadness or grief, a broken heart, or an attachment to someone, something or a particular outcome. By breathing into your heart center, you allow yourself to connect with your love and compassion and with opening your heart to yourself.

Throat Center

Move up to the "fifth chakra" or "throat center" by placing two fingertips in the little hollow right below the Adam's apple.

Exhale all air when you are ready. Take in a deep breath, filling the belly and the chest all the way up into the throat center.

On exhalation send the breath all the way down through your torso and out of the base center into the cushion of the chair.

Again breathe in all the way up into the throat center.

On exhalation send the breath down and out of the base center into the cushion.

Continue this breathing pattern.

The throat center is connected with our speaking voice as well as with speaking our voice—speaking our truth, knowing what we want, being able to ask for what we want, and being able to listen to ourselves and others. When we are energetically constrained in the throat center, we may experience a disconnect from our inner truth, not knowing what we want or not daring to ask for what we want, or not being able to listen to ourselves or to others. By breathing into your throat center, you allow yourself to connect with your inner truth, with what is so for you, and with your full, free self-expression.

Third-Eye Center

Place two fingertips on your "sixth chakra" or "third-eye center" in the middle of your forehead, above the eyebrows.

When you are ready, exhale all air.

Take in a deep breath, filling the belly and the chest all the way up into the third eye.

On exhalation send the breath all the way down through your torso and out of the base center into the cushion of the chair.

Again breathe all the way up into the third eye.

On exhalation send the breath down and out of the first center into the cushion.

Continue this breathing pattern.

The third-eye center is connected with our intuitive self and an ever-knowingness that goes far beyond what we have learned. By breathing into your third-eye center, you allow yourself to connect with the intuitive and ever-knowingness within yourself and everywhere.

Crown Center

Place your palm on the top of your head—the "seventh chakra" or "crown center."

When you are ready, exhale all air. Take in a deep breath, filling the belly and the chest all the way up to the top of the head.

On exhalation send the breath all the way down through your torso and out of the base center into the cushion of the chair.

Again breathe in, filling the belly and the chest all the way up to the top of the head.

On exhalation send the breath down and out of the first center into the cushion.

Continue this breathing pattern.

The crown center is connected with our spiritual self, the divine, and the eternal. By breathing into your crown center, you allow yourself to connect with the spiritual, the divine, and the eternal within you and everywhere.

Completing

Remove your hand and bring it back to your lap.

When you are ready, exhale all air.

Take in a deep breath from the bottom of your being, filling the belly and the chest all the way up to the top of the head.

On exhalation send the breath down like trickling water through the channel of your energy centers, all the way down and out of the base center and into the cushion of the chair, into the floor, into the earth.

Take one more deep breath in from the bottom to the top.

On exhalation send the breath down like trickling water through the channel of your energy centers, all the way down and out of the base center and into the cushion, into the floor, into the earth.

Continue breathing in your own rhythm, witnessing the

breath coming and going. Take a moment and notice how you feel. How is your body feeling? Any sensations or absence of sensations? Notice your emotional state. Then notice your state of mind.

Practice 3: Connect with Your Love Muscle
Pelvic-Floor Muscle Practice

Benefits
Increasing vitality and pleasant aliveness
Feeling grounded and centered in yourself
Maintaining healthy reproductive organs
Preventing incontinence in later years
Men:
Increased blood flow to the prostate gland
Allowing for separation of ejaculation from orgasm
Women:
Keeping the yoni healthy and well
Enhancing orgasmic capacity

Many of us find fitness an important part of our lives. We work out to be healthy and active. We make a point of eating well, jogging, or lifting weights to take care of our bodies and get the most out of our health.

The same is necessary for cultivating sexual enlightenment

and being intimately connected with oneself or another. There is a group of muscles that are important to exercise as part of increasing sexual fitness: the pubococcygeus muscle, or PC for short. It is also affectionately called the "love muscle."

The PC muscle group makes up and supports the pelvic floor of the body. In both men and women it serves important functions in supporting the inner organs including preventing incontinence, maintaining reproductive health, enhancing pleasurable sexual experiences, and allowing for the separation of ejaculation and orgasm for the man and increased aliveness of the yoni for the woman. Just like other muscle groups, the PC or love muscle needs to be worked to gain fitness. It can lose strength and toning during childbirth, lack of use, and simple aging.

The following practice will illustrate how to locate and gain control of your love muscle and use it to ground yourself in your body, heighten your sense of aliveness, and expand your solo and partner lovemaking to new levels of ecstasy.

To find your love muscle, imagine you are trying to stop the flow during urination and squeeze the muscle that would allow you to do so. Take a look at the images below to get a sense of the PC muscle group running through your pelvic floor.

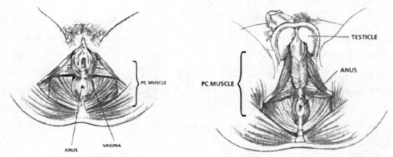

PC or Love Muscle—Female   PC or Love Muscle—Male

Jenny and Frank are a young, good-looking married couple who had lost their sex life. Both described being disgruntled and frustrated with sex, and Jenny stated she was just not that interested in it anymore and had given up. She explained that she almost never orgasmed during sex, and when asked if she ever faked orgasm, Frank scoffed and laughed. He said that he'd had no idea until recently that she had been faking her orgasms, and it upset him because he felt lied to. Jenny agreed it was the wrong thing to do.

The couple agreed to try the PC practices together, and during the exercise Jenny awoke something within herself. Her face became excited, and her cheeks blushed after using the squeeze and release technique with breath (see this practice at the end of this section). She giggled and looked to her husband, who was just as surprised as she was. Both felt encouraged.

The sensation of sexual energy sent Jenny into a fit of more giggles and fidgeting as she was clearly enjoying the pleasant sensations that were radiating in her sexual center. When asked what it felt like, Jenny looked down and, a bit shyly, said that it felt like she'd just had an orgasm. She sighed and giggled some more, saying that the sensations were weird but that she was clearly enjoying herself. As she breathed up her newfound sexual life-force energy, she looked alive and inspired. After more practice Jenny and Frank both were able to connect to their own and each other's sexual energy and experience greater fulfillment in their intimate and love life.

The first time Jenny did the PC practice, she was able to connect with sexual life-force energy and pleasure that she had been missing for years. Not everyone will have as profound an experience as she had, but there is certainly a lot to gain from bringing awareness and activity to the love muscle for both men and women. Some of the most basic benefits are an increased vitality and a pleasant aliveness as well as a feeling of being more grounded and centered in oneself. As a reminder the pelvic floor is the area where the first energy center (responsible for a sense of groundedness and security) and the second energy center (focusing on creativity and pleasure) reside.

This practice works to increase blood flow to the reproductive organs, and when there is more blood flow there is generally more oxygen, energy, and pleasure brought to the area as well. This can increase the flow of sexual hormones and work to maintain healthy organs such as the prostate and vagina.

Many women do PC exercises known as Kegels after pregnancy; these are almost identical to the practices below but without the conscious breath that adds energetic awareness, flow, and whole-body aliveness. The love muscle practice may open up new levels of attunement with a woman's body as well as her sensuous capacity. This can lead to greater joy and pleasure for her and her partner.

For the man, the mastery of this pelvic-floor muscle allows him to forgo the reflexive quivering of the PC muscle that occurs at a 9.5 on a scale of one to ten, where ten represents the climax or ejaculatory moment. Squeezing his love muscle right before the quivering occurs and coordinating the squeezing with his conscious breathing enables him to separate orgasm from ejaculation. By mastering the ejaculatory reflex, the man can sustain and circulate orgasmic energy as long as he chooses throughout his body, allowing him to stay present and connected to himself and his partner, deepening the sexual-spiritual connection.

Strengthening and gaining control of the PC muscle coordinated with conscious breath is a valuable technique for both sexes.

The Practice

Sit comfortably in a chair or on a cushion on the floor.

Squeezing and Releasing

Locate your PC muscle by squeezing as if you were holding back urination.

Release the muscle.

Take in a deep breath from the base center to the crown center.

On exhalation squeeze and release your PC muscle while

speaking the words "squeeze ... release ... squeeze ... release ... squeeze ... release."

At the bottom of the exhalation, take in a deep breath from the bottom to the top while continuing to squeeze and release your PC muscle.

Repeat the exercise for six inhalations and exhalations.

Relax the muscle and continue your own rhythm of breathing in and out.

Upon completion notice how you feel in the area you were squeezing and releasing.

Squeeze and release your PC muscle regularly during the day as you go about your normal activities. Start out with forty to fifty squeezes and releases. After a week increase the count to sixty, then to eighty, and after two weeks go up to one hundred. Increase to 150 times after three weeks of starting the practice. Notice how you feel and any changes that may occur for you.

Sustained Squeeze

Take in a deep breath through the nose. At the top of the breath, hold the air in and squeeze your PC muscle. Hold your breath for fifteen seconds.

Keep squeezing the PC muscle and slowly exhale with a "ssshhhh." At the bottom of the breath, release the squeeze of the PC muscle.

Repeat this pattern six more times.

Upon completion notice how you feel in the area you were squeezing and releasing.

Practice 4: Heart-to-Heart Connection
Partner Spooning Practice

Benefits
Coming into resonance with each other
Creating balance and harmony
Influencing the synchronicity between partners
Nurturing each other

The heart chakra constitutes the center point between the three upper and the three lower of the seven chakras. It reconciles our earthly existence with our spiritual beingness. It is the seat of the experience of universal and romantic love.

By practicing conscious awareness and connection with your own and your partner's heart center, you can open new experiences of love and intimacy as a couple. This practice builds upon the previously mentioned breathing techniques to broaden the mindful connection with a partner. Just as breath allows us to drop deeper into our bodies and ourselves, synchronized breath with another creates the same effect in both people.

Coming from the united heart center, a couple cultivates and connects in love. As we mentioned in chapter 6, the heart chakra is the place where we experience love, be it romantic or intimate love, love for ourselves, love for others, or universal love. When beloveds connect at the heart center, they find their balance within themselves and become present to each other by tuning at the same frequency. We drop out of our head, the busy mind, into our heart and love connection.

Rollin McCraty, the director of research at the Institute of HeartMath, wrote in *The Energetic Heart: Bioelectromagnetic Communication within and between People*, "The heart generates the largest electromagnetic field in the body. The electrical field as measured in an electrocardiogram (ECG) is about sixty times greater in amplitude than the brain waves recorded in an electroencephalogram (EEG)." He continues: "When people touch or are in proximity, a transference of the electromagnetic energy produced by the heart occurs."

We as humans have the capability to tune in to our own and each other's heart frequencies through bringing awareness to our feeling states.

In addition to synchronized breathing, this practice moves into a physical connection by having each partner place a hand on the other's heart center or connect heart center to heart center from the front or the back, as described in more detail in The Practice part at the end of this section. The physical connection coordinated with synchronized breathing facilitates the movement and flow of heart energy from one person to the other. It opens the flow of one partner's heart frequency to the other, which, with breath and visualization, can be circulated between the partners. Sharing heart energy with intention and attention removes barriers between the couple and opens the hearts to each other, allowing for love and intimacy to arise.

This practice can be used to alter the state of being to create a connection between a couple after a long day; before, during, and after lovemaking; and at any other time when you wish to transcend the commotion and reach a common ground and connection with each other.

Rita and Sam were in a relationship that was headed downhill after raising two young boys and working together in their joint business day after day. Sam described it as the passion having gone out of their relationship. Rita identified feeling disconnected and not like herself. The couple was proactive in their goal to rekindle their love, and after the first workshop at TantraNova they added the practices they had learned as an action item on their reconnection list!

Sam explained, "It isn't just about sex. It's about the connection. Particularly after we started the heart-to-heart connection practice, there was this *wow* moment, and everything started to turn around."

Rita agreed about the transformative experience of this practice. "We came back to our center in a few weeks. We couldn't stop talking with each other and holding hands, and we felt a great intimate connection."

Practicing conscious connection and breathing, Rita and Sam opened up to each other. "It has been a really good stress reliever for us," Rita said. "It feels easy and natural. We just melt into each other and find our way back to our mutual connectedness. This practice has been helping me calm down, relax, and connect with Sam, and I always end up feeling sexy and fulfilled."

Sam added, "We are one, not two separate people anymore. When we make love now, it's ten times more passionate."

When first doing the practice, Sam stated that he felt Rita's energy tingling from head to toe—he physically felt the energy washing over him. "You get to feel your partner—really feel her. And outside the bedroom, we are now best friends. We communicate more, have fun, and laugh. We're more open and trusting. We feel more complimentary, flowing, and natural."

The Practice

The couple lies together spoon-fashion on their left sides. The receiver on the inside is enveloped in the arms of the giver on the outside.

The giver, holding the receiver, has his or her left arm under the receiver's neck and his or her right hand resting on the receiver's heart chakra.

As you lie together, close your eyes and breathe together. The giver synchronizes his or her breath with the receiver's breath.

When exhaling, the giver visualizes sending love energy from his heart center into the receiver's heart center.

When inhaling, the giver receives love energy from the receiver's heart center in his or her right palm, and up his or her right arm and into the heart center.

Follow this breathing pattern for ten breaths.

Upon completion, switch roles.

Alternate breathing: you can also do this practice while one partner breathes in as the other partner breathes out.

Upon completion, face each other and gaze into each other's left eye. Breathe in and out together. Then share how you feel, how your body feels, and how you felt being the receiver or the giver. Make sure each of you gets to speak and to listen and that each of you is being listened to.

Eye gazing offers us a chance to get in tune with our partner, come to stillness, and be present to each other. Given that the left eye is correlated with the left brain hemisphere—the experiential, artistic, nonlinear part of the brain—we drop out of the judging and assessing state of mind into a feeling and sensing way of being that allows us to feel intimately connected. We no longer center on the idea of love but on the experience of love. This heart connection practice offers a chance to stop plucking flower petals and wondering if she or he loves you or not and instead actually experience the profound sense of love within and with each other.

Practice 5: Yin and Yang
Balancing Feminine and Masculine Energy Practice

Benefits
Integrating the feminine and masculine energies within
Coming to inner balance and peace

Throughout the practices in this book, we have illustrated the importance of peace and the power of harmony. This next exercise brings us to the balance between feminine and masculine energies that reside within each of us no matter our gender.

One of the universally recognized symbols of balance is the yin-yang image. The symbol illustrates the contrast of feminine (yin) and masculine (yang) energies as well the interdependence and ultimate wholeness as the two polarities are balanced and connected together. This phenomenon is happening in our bodies with our energy! This practice will bring awareness to both masculine and feminine energies as well as teach the steps needed for the feminine and masculine to dance and merge in harmony within our being.

Each of us, whether male, female, or somewhere on the spectrum between the two, experiences feminine and masculine energy—estrogen and testosterone. Feminine energy can be described as receptive, listening, creative, playful, or flowing while masculine energy can be described as linear, focused, intentional, or quick. The chart below further illuminates the characteristics of yang or masculine and yin or feminine. Take a look and locate yourself:

Characteristics and Expressions of Masculine (Yang) and Feminine (Yin) Principles

Masculine	Feminine
Sourced by the sky	Sourced by the earth
Spirit of inspiration; grounded vision	Spirit of generosity, grace, nurturing, and support
Creative focus	Creative flow
Purposeful presence	Open and connected
Desire for truth	Desire for sourcing and sustaining
Oriented toward vision and goals	Oriented toward love and care
In one's mind and focused	In one's emotions and flow
Persistent in direction	Listening and nurturing
Emotion of compassion	Emotions of trust and gratitude
Breaking free and winning	Loving and relating
Angular and linear	Flowing and circular
Self-disciplined	Sensitive and intuitive
Looking at life from the outside	Looking at life from within
Coming from thought and knowledge	Coming from feeling and empathy
Fear of failure in life	Fear of rejection and loss of love
Work before intimacy	Intimacy before work
Always involved in a mission or project	Always in the flow of giving and receiving love
Solving problems	Caring and reconciling
One's action mode can't be wrong—it just is	One's emotion mode can't be wrong—it just is
Doing	Being

Considering different areas of your life, you may find yourself more in one column than the other. At times you may find yourself in balance between the two columns or switching depending on the situation.

The yin-yang practice is useful for realigning ourselves when we get out of balance or when a more masculine or more feminine energy needs to be brought to the forefront of our being to assist in our daily functioning and relating. When we are balanced and connected with the feminine and masculine within ourselves, we are in tune with our creative power and ease.

Maria owns a life-coaching business and uses the yin-yang practice to balance her energy in the professional world. "Doing this practice regularly has expanded who I am as a professional. Until I was able to manage my energy, I could not manage my business effectively and live up to my full potential."

In order to be successful at doing business in a man's world, Maria felt she needed to take on that masculine energy. "I would find myself wearing stiff, formal suits and not getting that I could be productive while being guided by my feminine core." She started to realize that she felt off balance; she noticed tightness in her neck with a sense of being burdened, and she became aware of a lurking fear arising in her solar plexus.

Through this meditation practice, Maria became more and more aware of the discomfort in which she had been living. She started realigning herself, coming from a more grounded, centered place. "When I do the yin-yang practice, I just breathe into the tense spaces and let go, let it all go. I start to visualize my masculine and feminine energies swirling and dancing together as I consciously bring forth the integration of the feminine and masculine within myself."

The balanced blend of yin and yang energies allows us to respond to situations and needs differently, and when we become conscious of which energy space we would *like to* operate out of versus which one we *are* operating out of, we can make the necessary changes. For example, Maria reports that the masculine energy she calls on to run, drive, and produce her business is now balanced by the feminine enquiring, listening, open, and fluid space she chooses to come from when doing life-coaching and business-coaching sessions.

"Sometimes I choose to allow my feminine energy to flow in the best interest of the client," she explains. "I make space for their solutions and answers to a question or problem instead of coming up with the answer myself right away."

This can also be applied to other relationships and alliances. At times we may simply need to allow space for processing with a partner, and at others we may need to be assertive and take action to help solve a problem. With the awareness and balancing techniques we learn by doing the yin-yang practice, we have the power to act from both our masculine and feminine sides equally at any moment.

Maria adds, "When I am balanced and centered, I can be in the present moment and engage as needed.

The Practice

Sit on a meditation chair, a cushion, or a regular chair. Focus on your buttocks resting on the cushion, and let them relax.

Exhale all air. When you are ready, take in a deep breath, filling your belly like a big balloon.

On exhalation send the breath down and out of the base center into the cushion of the chair.

Take another deep breath in, filling your belly like a big balloon.

On exhalation send the breath down and out of the base center into the cushion.

With each exhalation notice your buttocks sinking farther into the cushion and letting go, relaxing.

Connection with the Earth—the Feminine or Yin Energy

Take a deep breath into the belly and up into the chest.

On exhalation guide the breath down and out of the first center into the cushion, all the way down into the earth.

When you breathe in, visualize breathing in from the earth

all the way up into your belly and on into the chest and the heart center.

On exhalation send the breath all the way down into the floor, into the earth.

Continue breathing in this pattern.

The earth is considered feminine, or yin, as far as energy is concerned. The feminine can be described as flowing, round, circular, slow, listening, receptive, playful, creative, soft, capricious, or being open.

With each inhalation breathe the feminine up from the earth into your body, up into your heart center.

On exhalation let it spread out from your heart center into your whole body, into every facet of your body.

Again breathe in the feminine energy from below, all the way up into your heart center.

Again on exhalation let it spread out from your heart center into your whole body, into every facet of your body.

Continue breathing in and out in this way.

Connection with the Sky—the Masculine or Yang Energy

Now bring your attention to the crown center.

On exhalation send the breath up and out of your crown center, all the way up through the ceiling and to the sky.

On inhalation breathe in from the sky through the crown of your head and into your heart center.

Again on exhalation send the breath up and out of your crown center, all the way up through the ceiling and to the sky.

Again on inhalation breathe in from the sky through the crown of your head and into your heart center.

Continue breathing in this pattern for four more breaths.

The sky is considered masculine, or yang, as far as energy is concerned. The masculine can be described as directional, straight, linear, quick, speaking, giving, grounded, intentional, strong, or focused.

On your next inhalation, breathe in the masculine from above, through your crown center and into your heart center.

On exhalation send the masculine energy from your heart center through your whole body, feeling it in every facet of your being.

Again on inhalation breathe in the masculine from above, through your crown center and into your heart center.

Again on exhalation send the masculine energy from your heart center through your whole body, feeling it in every facet of your being.

Continue breathing in and out in this pattern for four more breaths.

Integration of the Feminine and Masculine Energies

On your next inhalation breathe up from the earth, receiving the feminine from below, and down from the sky, receiving the masculine from above.

The feminine and masculine are meeting in your heart center, where they integrate like yin and yang.

From there, on exhalation, the integrated feminine and masculine permeate your whole body—a balanced dance of yin and yang, soft and strong, listening and speaking, receiving and giving, slow and quick, circular and linear, playful and grounded, creative and intentional. Let the feminine and the masculine dance together throughout your body.

Continue breathing in and out this way for five more breaths.

Completing

Take in a deep breath coming up from the earth, all the way through you and out of your crown center, up to the sky.

On exhalation send the breath from the sky all the way through your body, back down again into the earth.

Without any particular guidance, notice the axis that you are between the earth and the sky with energy flowing through you all the time. You are supported by the earth below and protected by the sky above.

Continue breathing in your own rhythm, letting the breath come and go.

Take a moment to notice how you feel. Notice how your body is feeling and any sensations or absence of sensations. Become aware of anything else that might be present for you at this very moment.

Slowly come back into the room by opening your eyes and reorienting yourself in the physical space.

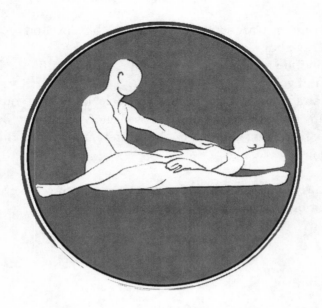

Practice 6: Sexual Healing Practices
Practices for the Woman and the Man

Benefits
For the woman: reawakening feminine energy and joy
For the man: sustaining masculine energy and pleasure
Releasing blocks from the past that no longer serve us

Sexuality and spirituality are two sides of the same coin—one would not exist without the other. Like yin and yang, where the white half of the image could not be distinguished without the black half, sexuality and spirituality are integrally related and as such are one. Our culture's separation of these two aspects may be an ill-conceived view and therefore counter to fostering well-being, health, and joy in our bodies, hearts, and spirits. When we bring conscious awareness to the integration of the sexual with the spiritual and the spiritual with the sexual, we return to a sense of wholeness within.

The TantraNova healing practices provide a rediscovery of our sexual-spiritual connection by teaching us how to clear blocks, residual memories, and views that no longer serve us and how to channel our life-force energy throughout our physical, emotional, and spiritual being. This allows for experiencing unity, joy, and harmony within oneself and with another and sets the stage for coming to sexual enlightenment.

So often we associate shame, fear, and guilt with sexuality and the sexual center. Sexual healing allows us to get in touch with, witness, explore, and ultimately release these constricting energies. The word *healing* is used here in terms of letting go of what keeps us from being fully integrated and whole.

Opportunities and Challenges

The healing rituals for the woman and the man illustrate what is possible for the individual and the couple. By using conscious touch and massage, eye gazing, communication, pressure points, and conscious breathing, the woman experiences a reawakening of her feminine energy and the man learns to channel and sustain his masculine energy. The healing practices enable each partner to connect with his or her own spiritual being while opening to his or her sexual life-force energy by integrating the aforementioned practices of pelvic-floor muscle activation, conscious breathing, and energy movement.

Sexual energy shows up in very different ways for women and men, leading to unique challenges and opportunities for each gender. Estrogen, the "slow hormone," is predominant in women, so their sexual energy rises slowly and gradually and then plateaus. The intention for the woman's healing is to reawaken feminine energy and joy. Through the healing the woman connects with her yoni, or "sacred space," and becomes more conscious of her sexual energy. She is able to get to know herself better and awaken her life-force energy. She can learn to take ownership of her sexuality and better convey what she wants or does not want from her partner.

The man's healing focuses on sustaining masculine energy and pleasure. Through it he becomes more conscious of his life-force energy and practices sustaining and channeling his aroused energy by breathing it up into his heart. He learns to use his powerful lingam or "magic wand" energy to imbue his heart center and love energy, which allows for deeper connection and intimacy within himself and with his partner.

Roles of Giver and Receiver

Creating a safe, sacred environment for the healing practice is essential. A particular structure is outlined for the ritual, which lays the foundation for trust and open communication. The roles of giver and receiver are assigned and maintained throughout the entire ritual, which allows for a unique experience. The receiver gets to receive fully without any expectation of having to give back.

When a woman allows herself to receive completely, a door opens to deeper connection and intimacy with herself and her partner. She may experience feeling "gotten" for who she is, or perhaps listened to for the first time without agenda or expectation. This in itself may provide a profound healing for her. The giver gives their full attention and presence to the receiver, assisting her in coming to a deeper listening to herself and her yoni or sacred space.

For the man, purely receiving without giving may be a challenge. Testosterone, the "quick hormone," is predominant in males and contributes to a more driving or outward nature—a characteristic of masculine energy we elaborated on previously in the Yin-Yang Practice. While this may be a welcomed capacity in many ways, it may be limiting if not balanced with the capacity to listen and receive, which are characteristics of the feminine energy. By allowing himself to drop into the receiver role, the man connects more consciously with his aliveness and range of subtle energies. He learns to become a witness of his orgasmic nectar without having to perform.

The healing practices are designed for heterosexual as well as same-sex couples. However, in our advanced women's workshops at TantraNova, we also guide women in how to be in the healer role with another woman. The nurturing, gentle, and intuitive dynamics of feminine-to-feminine energies can have most profound healing effects. In this particular arrangement, the woman giver is there as a kind of a midwife to the woman receiver. The important part is that the structure and roles are established and maintained and clear and open communication is present.

Healing for the Woman Practice

The healing practice for the woman—or the *yoni ritual*, as it's often called—may be experienced as something pleasant, connecting, and opening, or the receiver might get in touch with experiences from earlier times in her life that might trigger an emotional process. During her healing ritual, the woman is connecting to herself in the present moment. She is supported by a compassionate partner who holds space for her to work with and process whatever comes up. Energetic blocks, memories, or unpleasant feelings that may have been stored as residual memories on the cellular level of the yoni or vaginal walls may be released so healing can occur.

During the process it is important for the giver to remember not to take anything personally—not to try to fix her but to let her be and honor her, to encourage her to share more, and to listen to her and not to correct, interrupt, or solve. If tears are present, thank her for them. Remember, this quest is not about being sexual or having orgasms. It is about healing and reawakening the feminine, creative life-force energy.

When Kristy came to TantraNova, she had been afflicted by gynecological complications such as recurring yeast infections for many years, which made intercourse extremely painful. She shared that she felt like a "broken" woman and wanted to explore ways in which she could express her sexual self despite her physical concerns. She entered the TantraNova woman's healing workshop feeling nervous, uptight, scared to open up, and afraid to trust. When it came to choosing a partner for the homework healing practice, she partnered with a most supportive and attentive man. She experienced him as patient and felt that she could slowly open up and begin to trust.

The most impactful experience of the healing ritual was that for the first time Kristy felt her male partner was simply present with and for her, absent of any agenda of his own or expectations of her. Being in this space of acceptance and presence, she could let go of the guilt and shame connected with her yoni and release her sadness over and frustration with the pain she had been experiencing. Following the workshop she felt a sense of aliveness, an inner groundedness, and a newfound confidence she had not had before. To her great surprise, a lot of her physical pelvic pain subsided along with the frequent headaches that had plagued her.

Healing for the Man Practice

The man's healing practice offers techniques for sustaining sexual energy and for moving aroused energy up to the heart chakra and beyond. This practice can create awareness and empowerment for the man. He learns how to stay connected with his sexual-spiritual unity not just in a sexual encounter but throughout his day.

As a receiver the man focuses on giving his energy to himself, so to speak. Breathing is essential while using the contraction of his PC or love muscle to stave off the ejaculatory reflex; the man continuously breathes his life-force energy or orgasmic nectar up through the channel of his chakras and into his heart. The intention is to learn how to harness and master his sexual life-force energy instead of expelling it. This makes available a capacity to be and stay present to himself and his orgasmic energy as well as experience longer, full-body orgasms and sustained erections.

Working with his energy in this way is deeply empowering for the man. He is grounded in his manhood while open in his heart. Mastering his life-force energy extends to outside the bedroom. As mentioned before, sexual energy is creative—the root of all life. Any activity that is creative is based in this life-force energy. When it is transformed into heart energy, the man can use it to create more joy and abundance in his life; when he channels it into his third-eye center, his conscious being, he incites his intentions and visions to be nurtured into manifestation. Then he no longer merely reacts to the automatic biological urge. Rather he experiences a profound sense of wholeness within and connectedness to life itself.

Remember Jay from chapter 7 who spoke about becoming more conscious of his sexual life-force energy by starting to exercise and master his ejaculatory reflex? This in turn enabled him to channel his orgasmic energy up into his heart and third-eye centers. He said, "By doing the pelvic-floor muscle squeeze, I ignite my sexual energy and can feel it stir my lower chakras. It's the sensation that awakens arousal and desire. Through practice, focus, and guided breath, I am now able to channel the arousal throughout my whole being. This allows me to sustain and connect more deeply with myself solo or with my beloved in partner sex. It also allows me to transmute that vital and pleasant energy into my acting career and goals."

When a man channels and transforms his sexual energy into love energy, he can meet his partner at her heart. By transmuting lust into heart-loving ecstasy, he can be truly present to himself and his partner. Lovemaking becomes no longer about the end goal but about experiencing the present moment of bliss and joy. Sexual or life-force energy becomes the channeled spark through which he fuels himself and his life in and outside the bedroom.

Practical Learning

These powerful healing practices offer a model for creating a sexy-Zen state of being, experiencing, and healing for both partners as they give or receive. For practical, hands-on instruction of the healing rituals, please take a look at the TantraNova DVD called *The Discovery of Sexual-Spiritual Connection* listed in the Resources section at the end of this book.

Chapter 11
Sexual Enlightenment Starts Now!

Practice creates the master.
—Don Miguel Ruiz, *The Mastery of Love*

Now that you have read this book and given yourself a solid background on the theoretical and practical aspects of sexual enlightenment, the only thing left is for you to begin your journey. Armed with the insight and knowledge you have gained up until this point; the awareness you have begun to cultivate through acknowledging and perhaps beginning to examine the way you view your sexual life-force energy; and a curiosity about and a willingness to explore your relationship with yourself, with your beloved if you are in a relationship, or with others in your life, you may find this a rewarding path to follow. Sexual enlightenment is, after all, a lifelong exploration— the journey itself will undoubtedly change the way you think, feel about, and engage with yourself, your relationships, your work, your means of expression, and every other aspect of life as you know it.

Taking the first step toward sexual enlightenment may be an exciting undertaking for some but a daunting and frightening leap for others. Just imagine what you may clear in the process, perhaps blocks that hold you back or illusions or cognitive blindness that have you repeating the same pattern or behavior over and over again. Most importantly, think about how you may be able to create and bring effortlessly into your life what you want at this time and in doing so, open yourself up to a more creative, more passionate, and more joyful life.

You Hold the Keys

Producing change or expansion in one's life is a process that can be different for each person who chooses to undertake it. Some might find it to be simple and quick while for others it might be quite lengthy and complex, with many layers that must be unfolded before the change can become visible.

However, there are two key aspects you'll need to include for a successful journey to transforming yourself and your life no matter what the timeline.

- Shift your mindset! As we lay out in this book, a new view of sexual energy is required that will open new vistas and possibilities for a fulfilled life individually and collectively. This view goes far beyond the mere biological purpose of procreation, beyond the mere satisfaction of carnal desires and infatuations, and beyond simply sex in the bedroom. It allows us to see that sexual energy is the spark of life that fuels everything. With that awareness we open ourselves to drawing on and transmuting that spark, which is creative and joyous in nature, as a source for creating our lives, relationships, professions, and communities.

- Practice, practice, practice! Just as it is with anything else we attempt, without regular practice nothing will change and evolve. Take the practices we introduced in chapter ten and implement them into your daily routine by yourself and/or with your partner. Recurrent practice will allow you to face what may be in the way of experiencing fulfillment. Remember, sexual enlightenment is not a "one and done" event; it shows up in the process of life itself as an experience, an insight, and a sense of wholeness within. Continued practice will usher you through this process like a lighthouse aids maritime pilots navigating at sea.

People frequently ask us, "How long does it take to become proficient in the practice?" Our answer is simple yet may be a great challenge to some: perfection is in the perfecting; the mastery resides in the ongoing pursuit and engagement. Just as Don Miguel Ruiz said in the quote at the top of this chapter, "Practice creates the master," and we cannot stress enough how important it is, when working toward your own sexual enlightenment, to be persistent and consistent in your practice. Along the way, as you practice, you may discover and uncover the subtleties, joys, and pearls that are only available with ongoing engagement with, dedication to, and pursuit of integrating yourself as a sexual-spiritual being. And as with any other practice, eventually you will find your rewards: in this case, the experience of fulfillment, presence, and happiness in your life and your relationships.

To Be Is to Do

Aristotle said, "For the things we have to learn before we can do them, we learn by doing them," and from the time of the ancient Greeks until today it has held true. So many things in life come to us only when we take that first step and embark on the journey— we learn as we go. We can write about sexual energy and sexual enlightenment, and we can introduce practices; we can describe what it feels like for a person to clear energy blocks from their body; and we can give you advice on how to do this for yourself and how it could better your life.

However, nothing truly takes the place of actual experience. Hence you will learn more about yourself and your journey toward sexual enlightenment by immersing yourself in that process and allowing yourself to feel it with all of your senses. You will discover what works best and is most effective for you by entering into the practice.

Here are some effective suggestions that you can start with right away:

- Connect daily with your conscious belly breath: when you wake up, when sitting at your desk at work, during a heated conversation with a friend or a beloved—whenever you need to remind yourself to come back to yourself in the present moment or feel you need to center and ground yourself.

- Become the watcher and witness of your thoughts and feelings. Do this with no judgment or approval of what you think and feel. Look at them as if you were watching a movie and decide if these thoughts or feelings are serving you or not—then choose if you want to perpetuate them or let them go.

- Do something you love every day. Dance around your house; sit quietly and practice conscious breathing; play music; have an inspiring conversation; work in your garden; laugh often; appreciate yourself and others in your life; or do whatever you know will bring you joy.

Incorporating these three suggestions into your daily life will give you a good start and will lay the foundation for your practice of experiencing sexual enlightenment. The detailed Resources section following this chapter will further assist you in bringing the TantraNova practices into your life and relationships by putting yourself on the path to lasting fulfillment in life, love, and intimacy.

Resources

Free Download of Chapter 10: Practices

To support you in establishing and doing your daily practices, we have made available a free download of the first five practices we detailed in chapter 10. To access the five practices, please visit http://www.tantranova.com/foundational-practices.html.

The sixth practice from chapter 10, "Sexual Healing Practices—Practices for the Woman and the Man," is available on our advanced-level DVD called *The Discovery of Sexual-Spiritual Connection.*

To acquire the DVD or to download: http://www.tantranova.com/intimacy-products/tantranova-products/intimacy-dvds.html

Home-Study Program—available on DVD and CD as well as via download.

If you cannot join us at TantraNova for a workshop, or if you want to prepare ahead of time for attending one of our live workshops or private programs, our home-study program is an ideal way of learning and getting involved. Start with our beginner-level *Creating Intimacy & Love* DVD as an introduction to the TantraNova work and do one or more of the practices from our *TantraNova Foundational Practices* CD daily. Once you have laid a foundation, you can move on to our advanced *The Discovery of Sexual-Spiritual Connection* DVD, where you will be guided in the sexual healing practices for the woman and the man via a practical, hands-on approach. You can find all of these media available at http://www.tantranova.com/intimacy-products/tantranova-products/intimacy-dvds.html.

After years of practice, we at TantraNova still prefer to be guided in our daily practice by listening to the *TantraNova Practices* CD, which assists us in staying present and coming back more easily from the intermittent chatter of the mind that we become so aware of during times of stillness and conscious breathing. It also ensures that we achieve the fullest results from our daily practice.

Live Workshops, Retreats, and Private Programs

While one person may embark on the sexual enlightenment journey by himself or herself, we have found in our own lives and while assisting thousands of couples and singles that there is nothing like working with a coach. While we can learn from books, movies, talks, and the like, the guidance of an experienced and seasoned teacher can be the difference between achieving breakthrough results in record time and moving at a snail's pace, remaining stagnant, or giving up on oneself.

From experience we know that the most effective and fastest way to take on a new endeavor, learn about a new field, or develop a new skill is to work with a coach who knows what he or she is doing. This relationship allows us to learn in action like players on a sporting field; it puts us on the court rather than in the stands as passive spectators. A coach or mentor with a different perspective and purview than one's own can be an experienced voice to show us the blind spots in our views, interpretations, behaviors, or approaches that we cannot see for ourselves; even minute interventions on a coach's part can allow for quantum shifts in the way we approach the game and become successful in our practice and the subsequent results we produce.

We at TantraNova offer this teacher's or coach's role via group workshops, retreats, and private programs. Go to our program page on the TantraNova.com website to learn more about each platform and to find out which offering may support you best at this time in your life: http://www.tantranova.com/intimacy-programs/intimacy-tantra-programs.html.

TantraNova Resources at a Glance

FREE TantraNova Practices Audio Download
http://www.tantranova.com/foundational-practices.html
Practice 1   Calm the Unending Chatter in Your Mind:
            Conscious Breathing Practice
Practice 2   Circulating Energy: Chakra Listening Practice
Practice 3   Connect with Your Love Muscle: Pelvic-Floor
            Muscle Practice
Practice 4   Heart-to-Heart Connection: Partner Practice
Practice 5   Yin and Yang: Balancing Feminine and
            Masculine Energy Practice

FREE 10 Essential TantraNova Practices
http://www.tantranova.com/
Opt-in on home page and receive the free Print Download:
"Creating Intimacy & Love"

TantraNova Home-Study Course: Introduction to Sexual Healing Practices
http://www.tantranova.com/intimacy-products/intimacy-dvds.html
DVD Volume I: *Creating Intimacy & Love*
DVD Volume II: *The Discovery of Sexual-Spiritual Connection*
Audio CD: *TantraNova Foundational Practices*

Youth Program
http://www.bringforthyouth.com/
Empowerment and Leadership Program for Teens

Other Resources

We would like to share with you additional resources that assisted us on our journey. May they assist you as well!

Bibliography

Austin, John Langshaw, *How to Do Things with Words*, Cambridge, MA: Harvard University Press, 1975.

Brach, Tara. *True Refuge: Finding Peace and Freedom in Your Own Awakened Heart*, New York: Random House, 2013.

Canfield, Jack. *The Success Principles: How to Get from Where You Are to Where You Want to Be*, New York, NY: HarperCollins Publishers, 2006.

Eisler, Riane, PhD. *The Power of Partnership: Seven Relationships that Will Change Your Life*, Novato, CA: New World Library, 2003.

Flores, Fernando and Maria. *Conversations For Action and Collected Essays: Instilling a Culture of Commitment in Working Relationships*, CreateSpace, 2013.

Hill, Napoleon. *Think and Grow Rich*, Wise, VA: Napoleon Hill Foundation, 2012.

Huxley, Julian. "Transhumanism" in *New Bottles for New Wine*, London: Chatto & Windus, 1957.

Lama, Yeshe. *Introduction to Tantra*, Somerville, MA: Wisdom Publications, 2001.

Marx Hubbard, Barbara. *Birth 2012 and Beyond: Humanity's Great Shift to the Age of Conscious Evolution*, Chicago, IL: Shift Books, 2012.

McCraty, Rollin. *The Energetic Heart: Bioelectromagnetic Interactions Within and Between People*, Boulder Creek, CA: The Institute of HeartMath.

Osho. *Sex Matters*, New York, NY: St. Martin's Press, 2002.

Ruiz, Don Miguel, *The Mastery of Love: A Practical Guide to the Art of Relationship: A Toltec Wisdom Book*, San Rafael, CA: Amber-Allen Publishing, 1999.

Searle, John Rogers. *Speech Acts: An Essay in the Philosophy of Language*, Cambridge, UK: Cambridge University Press, 1970.

Tolle, Eckhart. *The Power of Now: A Guide to Spiritual Enlightenment*, Novato, CA: New World Library, 2004.

Tolle, Eckhart. *A New Earth: Awakening to Your Life's Purpose*, New York, NY: Penguin, 2008.

Weaver, Fred. *Creative Self Discovery: A Journey into Self-Consciousness*, Bloomington, IN: Xlibris Corp, 2000.

Williamson, Marianne. *A Return to Love: Reflections on the Principles of "A Course in Miracles,"* New York, NY: HarperOne, 1996.

For the Couple

Chia, Mantak and M. Chia. *The Multi-Orgasmic Couple*, New York, NY: Harper Collins, 2000.

Long, Barry. *Making Love: Sexual Love the Divine Way*, Queensland, AU: Barry Long Books, 1998.

Muir, Charles and Caroline. *Tantra: The Art of Conscious Loving*, San Francisco, CA: Mercury House, 1989.

For Men

Chia, Mantak. *Taoist Secrets of Love: Cultivating Male Sexual Energy*, Santa Fe, NM: Aurora Press, 1984.

Riley, Kerry and Diane. *Tantric Secrets for Men: What Every Woman Will Want Her Man to Know about Enhancing Sexual Ecstasy*, Rochester, VT: Destiny Books, 2002.

For Women

Chia, Mantak. *Cultivating Female Sexual Energy*, Thailand: Healing Tao Books, 1986.
Carrellas, Barbara. *Urban Tantra: Sacred Sex for the Twenty-First Century*, Berkeley, CA: Celestial Arts, 2007.
Taylor, Susan, PhD. *Sexual Radiance: A 21-Day Program of Breathwork, Nutrition, and Exercise for Vitality and Sensuality*, New York, NY: Harmony Books/Crown, 1998.

Websites

Dr. Michael Bernard Beckwith: http://www.agapelive.com/.
Eckhart Tolle: http://www.eckharttolle.com/.
Esalen Institute, Big Sur, CA: http://www.esalen.org/.
Kripalu Center for Yoga and Health, Lenox, MA: http://www.kripalu.org/.

Glossary

Energy:

Energy is ever present in all that is alive as well as all that is inert. In essence everything is energy manifesting in different forms at different times. For example, it can show up as physical matter such as the floor beneath the chair on which you sit. Or it can be a liquid such as the water in your drinking glass, or even a gas such as the air you breathe. It all depends on the density and frequency of the energy.

Life-force energy brings forth life. Its purpose is self-evident. It makes sense then that it will be present only in forms that contain life themselves and are fueled by that innate energy. There is no life force in inert states such as gases, or in non-living objects such as rocks.

Sexual energy and life-force energy are one and the same. This energy is an undercurrent that has always existed; without sexual energy none of us would be here. Sexual energy in its physical manifestation and experience is unique in that it's creative and pleasurable.

Consciousness:

Sexual enlightenment: We consider sexual enlightenment to be distinguished by two dimensions. The first involves sexual life-force energy that brings forth life in all that is alive—human beings, animals, and plants. The second dimension of sexual enlightenment involves the human capacity to be self-reflective or aware of one's own existence, particularly becoming aware and conscious of one's life-force energy that is sexual in nature.

Consciousness on both the individual and collective levels has to do with how the world occurs to us and how possibilities are open or closed to us. It provides the context for what drives our actions and behaviors.

Universal consciousness: When we say *universal consciousness*, we speak of the ever-present force that exists—and has always existed—within and around us throughout the infinite universe. Sexual energy is a manifestation of universal consciousness that has been creating, sustaining, and expanding life for billions of years.

Sex consciousness: Bringing consciousness to sexual energy enables us to channel and transmute sexual life-force energy in and outside of the bedroom. In this light we expand on the interpretation of sex, focusing on creativity, joy, and pleasure as a result of consciously connecting with our sexual life-force energy no matter if it shows up in the act of lovemaking or in the activities of our everyday lives.

Conscious evolution implies the shift from *evolution by chance to evolution by choice* as brought forward by Barbara Marx Hubbard. In the context of this book it is the possibility of shifting from being unconsciously at the effect of sexual energy— or our biology—to consciously choosing to evolve ourselves through this energy.

Sexual-spiritual: Sexuality and spirituality are two sides of the same coin—one would not exist without the other. Like yin and yang, where the white half of the image could not be distinguished without the black half, sexuality and spirituality are integrally related and as such are one. When we bring conscious awareness to the integration of the sexual with the spiritual or the spiritual with the sexual, we return to a sense of wholeness within.

Observer or witness: The observer or witness state of mind refers to our human ability to be self-reflective or aware of our own existence—also called the *observer of the self.*

Love:

Romantic love: The characteristic of romantic love is that it's conditional—that is, we experience these feelings we know as love for another person as long as that person is pleasing to us and is loving us back.

Unconditional love can be best illustrated as between a parent and a child. For example, unconditional love is present no matter how the child or teenager behaves. This form of love may appear at times as "tough love" yet is always in the context of *being love.*

Universal love implies a strong commitment to oneself and a vow to honor, respect, and care for the well-being of another person no matter what situations arise. It is an awareness that allows us to see ourselves in each other and to truly feel the oneness of humankind. We evolve into sustaining love as a practice versus a temporary state of feeling.

Traditions:

Generative language: Language is generative in nature versus merely descriptive, as pointed out in speech act theory in the philosophy of language based on John Langshaw Austin's and John Rogers Searle's work in the 1950s and '60s respectively and made further accessible—beyond academia—to business and organizational environments by Fernando Flores in the 1980s.

Creative self-discovery: To enhance the access to creativity and pleasure, we make use of music, movement, and drama as developed in creative self-discovery by Fred Weaver III, MD, in the latter part of the twentieth century.

Tantra is a tradition that originated in India more than five thousand years ago. It teaches sexual practices not only as a means of physical arousal but also to bring attunement and harmony to oneself and to one's relationships and facilitate heightened states of awareness. This was a highly spiritual endeavor that allowed for an experience of spiritual-sexual oneness and connectedness.

Taoism: The ancient Taoists in China thousands of years ago considered that performing "the bedroom arts," as they called them, could help one to stay in good health and increase longevity. As far back as the Han Dynasty, some Taoist secrets referred to intercourse as "joining energy" and treated it as a sacred, spiritual practice. They believed conscious lovemaking allowed for harnessing sexual energy in order to replenish life force.

About the Authors

Dr. Elsbeth Meuth and Freddy Zental Weaver are the founders and directors of the TantraNova Institute in Chicago. They are internationally renowned workshop leaders, relationship and intimacy coaches, and certified Tantra yoga teachers.

Their retreats and workshops have been offered throughout the United States, Canada, Europe and Australia. They are the producers of the bestselling DVD series *Creating Intimacy & Love* and were featured on Showtime's documentary series *Sexual Healing* and the Emmy award-winning NBC show *Starting Over.*

Elsbeth and Freddy Zental have assisted more than ten thousand couples and singles in rekindling and expanding their love and relationships. They are on the faculty at Esalen in Big

Sur, California, and at Kripalu in Stockbridge, Massachusetts. They lead couples' retreats for CEOs and their spouses/partners through the Young Presidents Organization (YPO) and have received the highest recognition for their work.

Elsbeth and Freddy Zental are sought-after speakers who have presented at Loyola University; Northwestern University; University of Chicago, Illinois Association for Marriage & Family Therapy; The American School of Professional Psychology of Argosy University; and Bodhi Spiritual Center.

Elsbeth has served as a doctoral dissertation advisor in the past. The efficacy of Dr. Elsbeth Meuth's and Freddy Zental Weaver's work is captured in the 2009 doctor of psychology research thesis "The Impact of Tantra on Couples' Intimacy and Sexual Experience" by Meredith E. McMahon of The American School of Professional Psychology of Argosy University, Chicago.

Elsbeth Meuth, EdD, was born and raised in Germany and has been developing her career over the past forty years in the United States and Europe. As a management consultant and executive coach at Business Design Associates, a firm founded by Dr. Fernando Flores, she worked with clients in the United States, Canada, and Europe. Elsbeth holds a doctorate in education and a master's degree in music. Her academic career includes associate professorships at Musikhochschule Nordrhein-Westfalen in Germany, and Berklee School of Music in Boston. She was a research fellow at the University of Indiana, Indianapolis, and is trained as an ontological design coach employing the principles of speech act theory and Heideggerian worldview.

Freddy Zental Weaver co-led creative self-discovery seminars at the Institute for Creative Living in Los Angeles, San Diego, San Francisco, and Hawaii. He employs the creative self-discovery approach as developed by psychiatrist and author Fred Weaver, MD. During Freddy Zental's tenure in software sales, he consistently achieved outstanding sales and income objectives.

Freddy Zental has served as a teacher and district-wide human relationship counselor in the Los Angeles Unified School District and is a performing artist with a one-man show called *Sexual Enlightenment* currently touring the United States. He is an accomplished percussionist, a stand-up comedian, and a storyteller who uses humor, music, and movement in his presentations and trainings. He holds a bachelor's degree in political science and is a certified Thai bodyworker.

Elsbeth and Freddy Zental are beloveds—life and business partners—residing in Chicago.